FOUL PLAY

FOUL PLAY

WHAT'S WRONG WITH SPORT

Joe Humphreys

ICON BOOKS

Published in the UK in 2008 by
Icon Books Ltd, The Old Dairy, Brook Road,
Thriplow, Cambridge SG8 7RG
email: info@iconbooks.co.uk
www.iconbooks.co.uk

Sold in the UK, Europe, South Africa and Asia
by Faber & Faber Ltd, 3 Queen Square,
London WC1N 3AU or their agents

Distributed in the UK, Europe, South Africa and Asia
by TBS Ltd, TBS Distribution Centre, Colchester Road
Frating Green, Colchester CO7 7DW

This edition published in Australia in 2008
by Allen & Unwin Pty Ltd, PO Box 8500,
83 Alexander Street, Crows Nest, NSW 2065

Distributed in Canada by Penguin Books Canada,
90 Eglinton Avenue East, Suite 700,
Toronto, Ontario M4P 2YE

ISBN: 978-1840468-90-8

CONTENTS

Joe Humphreys is an Irish journalist and author. He started out in newspapers as a racing tipster but quit after three months, having failed to predict a single winner. He subsequently worked as a reporter in news and sport in Ireland and South Africa, and is currently an assistant news editor with *The Irish Times*. His first book, *The Story of Virtue: Universal Lessons on How to Live*, which explores the teachings of world religions, received widespread praise. Married with one child, he holds a MA in Political Philosophy, supports West Ham United, and lives in Dublin.

Acknowledgements

I am very grateful to Professor Aidan Moran, director of the Psychology Research Laboratory, University College Dublin, for helping me wade through the body of sports psychology literature. Thanks also to his colleagues Kate Kirby and Tadhg MacIntyre.

Neville Cox, lecturer in law at Trinity College Dublin (and a Manchester United fan) was very helpful in discussing aspects of doping in sport. Paul Gleeson (Tottenham Hotspur) provided some excellent comments on a first draft of the book, while my brother Frank Humphreys (more of a tennis man than a footie fan) helped me to tidy up certain chapters.

Icon Books' Publishing Director, Simon Flynn (Everton FC) provided invaluable advice and recommendations, as did Editorial Director Duncan Heath. Their encouragement made writing this book a pleasure. I'm grateful too to Peter Pugh, Andrew Furlow, Sarah Higgins, Nick Sidwell and everyone else at Icon Books who has helped me to realise this project.

Sincere thanks also to *The Irish Times*, and the newspaper's editor Geraldine Kennedy, for facilitating my temporary relocation to South Africa in 2006–07, a move which afforded me the opportunity to write this book.

To my parents, Richard and Deirdre, and my other brothers, Richard and Mark, I'm so grateful for your support. Thanks Dad, in particular, for taking me to all those race-meetings when I was younger; the memories are special.

Last but not least, thanks to Emer for tolerating my various sporting passions down the years, and to Megan (by birth West Ham Utd) who has little time for what she calls 'silly old football' but has generously allowed me to dress her on special occasions in claret and blue.

For Emer

INTRODUCTION

'Absolutely devastated. Devastated. I couldn't believe my ears. I can't get over it.'

The caller was from Cork, in southern Ireland. He had heard the news just an hour beforehand. Like many of his ilk, his first thought was to ring pop broadcaster Joe Duffy and share his pain with the nation. Pat, the man's name was. He had kept the faith for 50 years, since 'before the Munich disaster'. But now he was having doubts. He couldn't have sounded more forlorn and despondent if he'd found the local bishop sleeping with his wife.

Duffy sympathised, wondering aloud whether Pat would remain in the fold.

'Unlikely,' Pat sighed.

'It's actually a nightmare here,' confided another Corkonian who phoned *Liveline*, Ireland's most-listened-to chat radio show, on that wintry afternoon in late 2005. (Remember, remember, the 18th of November?) 'The people are just in shock ... shock ... shock.' The voice trailed off in a shivery whimper. It was how a Russian peasant might have reacted to word of Lenin's death.

'We had a man on the phone at ten-to-one and he was bawling his eyes out,' said Duffy, fuelling the sense of national grief and bewilderment. 'It's the children I'm

1

upset for now, coming out of school at half-two, half-three.' Duffy urged parents to break the news gently ...

Roy Keane had left Manchester United by mutual consent.

———

Sport has an uncanny ability to make us lose perspective. We curse. We cheer. We scream. We cry. And then we wonder what all the fuss was about.

I often think of Pat, the 'devastated' Manchester United fan. I picture him in his local boozer, wearing the latest Red Devils replica jersey. (Despite all his talk of rebellion, you just know he wouldn't abandon his 'church'.) He's telling people how upset he was when Keane – who also happens to be from Cork – left the club, and then he blushes. He must blush, surely! No one can be devastated by another person's career move, especially when that person is just leaving one heavily-commercialised soccer franchise for another.

And yet, Pat's sorrow over the Keane affair is understandable. Understandable and, indeed, necessary for the world of sport as we know it to survive. After all, there can be no sport – no Sky Sports, no pull-out sports supplements, no merchandising of sport, no marketing, nor promoting, nor selling of sport – unless people take what is essentially a triviality seriously. For sport to flourish we need more Pats, especially the kind of Pat who spends as much as possible on trips to Old Trafford, and likes to pass his time reading *Shoot* magazine instead of *Private Eye*.

This is the paradox of sport. To enter its world, you must debase yourself. You must stupefy yourself. You must engage in various convoluted rituals (not unlike religion – but we'll come to that in a moment). At the same time, you must be earnest about your affiliation. To be a part of sport, you must believe the unbelievable. You must embrace your delusion. You must have faith.

This book is about that faith. It's a faith which I have shared as a lifelong sports fan, and as a player of sports (of very limited ability). The book is, therefore, part-confessional. It's an attempt to make sense of something that has been dear to me – often against logic – for as long as I can remember. But this book is also a critique of the broader sporting world, and particularly sport as it's played, watched, gambled upon or otherwise exploited today.

Take 18 November 2005 as our starting point. Keane left Manchester United and 70 people died in a bombing in Iraq. No prizes for guessing what led Ireland's main evening news. Iraq didn't even make second billing. That went to a report on the deteriorating health condition of an ex-footballer who hadn't played in serious competition for 30 years.

George Best wouldn't die for another full week. But that didn't stop him – or rather reports of his state of health – occupying thousands of hours of air time, and countless inches of newspaper space in the interim. Britain's tabloids were monitoring Best's up-down condition so closely that they felt confident enough to publish tribute supplements on the morning of his death, knowing he would breathe his last around then. Not even the death of Pope John Paul II a few months earlier generated such clamour in the press, nor such haste in rolling out eulogies for the deceased.

The hoopla surrounding Best's death was odd for a number of reasons. The Belfast man may well have been a brilliant footballer but he was relatively unknown outside of the UK and the Republic of Ireland, where his sporting legacy was overshadowed by a lifelong struggle with alcoholism. As *The Economist* magazine put it: 'Academics researching the social history of Britain in the second half of the 20th century may perhaps grant him [Best] the immortality of a footnote.' Why, then, the pull-out supplements? And the live, televised funeral? More to the point, why was the darker side of Best's life brushed over? Commentators, especially those from the football fraternity, repeated the mantra: 'He will be remembered for his football; everything else will be forgotten.' But would it really? It was Best's addiction to drink that killed him in the end. Denying his wasted years of abuse would be a reckless act of censorship.

A few weeks after Best's funeral, I was prompted to further reflect on the relationship between sports fans and their playing heroes. Paolo Di Canio, the Italian footballer who was then employed by Lazio, made a raised-arm salute to his club's notoriously right-wing 'Ultra' supporters at the end of a match in Livorno. The Lazio fans, some of whom brandished a swastika flag during the politically-charged game, had been 'goaded' throughout by the home team supporters' singing of anti-fascist songs.

Di Canio had been fined a few months earlier for making a raised arm salute at a Rome derby. Still, he was unapologetic. 'I saluted my people with what for me is a sign of belonging to a group that holds true values, values of civility against the standardisation that this society imposes upon us,' he said. 'If we are in the hand of the Jewish community it's the end. If action is taken because one community is up in arms it could be dangerous.'

The episode was an uncomfortable one for me. You see, I had always liked Paolo Di Canio. For four footballing seasons he had been the star player of 'my team', West Ham United. His bravado and over-the-top theatrics were what made him endearing, as much as his undoubted skill with the ball. I knew he had some dodgy views. I had read his autobiography in which he described Benito Mussolini as 'basically a very principled, ethical individual'. I knew – sure, it was there staring me in the face – that one of his arms had been tattooed with the word 'Dux' in honour of Italy's fascist dictator. Yet I chose to ignore it. As long as he kept scoring for the Hammers, I reasoned, what did I care?

Former team-mates of Di Canio expressed shock at the Livorno episode. But how could anyone have been surprised? Di Canio's behaviour was entirely in keeping with what had gone before. And that made me squirm because I used to cheer, if not act as cheerleader for, this buffoon who was prone to displays of extreme political incorrectness.

Ask anyone whose faith in God has been shaken when exactly they started having doubts and they'd be hard pressed to answer. It can rarely be traced to one thing, one event, or one betrayal. The same goes for my faith in sport. I cannot say when I started doubting myself. Nor can I speak of a Road-to-Damascus-like conversion. But I can confess that in the weeks surrounding 18 November 2005 I felt something had to give. Di Canio's fall from grace. The eulogising of Best. The hyping of the Keane affair. Against this backdrop, I asked myself: How, in God's name, did I ever get into sport in the first place?

The short answer is that I was born into it, like I was born into Christianity. Arguably, sport has retained a stronger grip since. Barely a day has passed in the last twenty years without some reading from The Back Pages, the ever-changing gospel of the sports fan. On the Seventh Day, oft bespoken of as Sky Super Sunday, I would worship at the altar of the Premier League. Likewise on Holy Days of Obligation, otherwise known as West Ham match fixture dates. Fidelity to my wife. Rearing my daughter. These were negotiables in my life. But missing a major

Irish international soccer fixture? Or copping out of a regular five-a-side game with fellow believers? No way; never! I had to do my absolutions, and God damn it, I wouldn't feel guilty about it – even if it meant disrupting a wedding anniversary or a birthday celebration.

Faith comes before family; the Buddha said that. Jesus too.

I was – and am – a product of my environment, of course. My faith was not fancied up from thin air but fuelled by the hot air of sports promoters. If the religious analogy can be stretched further, I might say that I grew up in an era in which the Sports Bar replaced the Sacristy, and the post-match analyst replaced the priest. Since the late 1980s, Mass attendances in 'Holy Catholic' Ireland have been decreasing almost in direct proportion to the rising demand for Manchester United, Liverpool, and, more lately, Sunderland tickets. In 2005, a World Cup qualifying game between the Republic of Ireland and Switzerland attracted almost twice as many Irish viewers as Pope John Paul II's funeral.

In Britain, 4.2 million people tuned in to the BBC's coverage of Mexico vs. Iran, an unglamorous group stages game during the 2006 World Cup. Some 4.2 million tuned into Holland vs. Serbia and Montenegro, broadcast by the BBC earlier the same day – a summer Sunday. Now compare that to the 2.5 million average weekly audience for *Songs of Praise* – a programme that used to be the lynchpin of the BBC's broadcasting schedule on the Sabbath.

As well as muscling in on traditional worshipping patterns, sport is increasingly appropriating the language of religion. Without irony, athletes are spoken of as gods, and golf shots as miracles. The Olympics, and other such international sporting events, are imbued with a supposed power to unite the peoples of the earth, and bring peace and harmony and goodwill, etc., in a way only the Man Above used to be able to. 'What is soccer if not everything that religion should be?' wrote one sports journalist on the eve of the 2006 Fifa World Cup. Rhetoric like this is as commonplace today as grace-before-meal was twenty years ago.

Such similarities between religion and contemporary sport can be regarded as trivial. But there is another parallel between the two forms of worship that cannot be ignored. This is their open embracing of mythology, or unreason. Like Christianity, Islam and Buddhism, sport has its foundational stories, or creation tales. These include the legend that sport was born of Corinthian purity and has since been sullied by 'unsporting' professionalism, and the related myth that sport 'builds character', turning waifs and delinquents into pillars of society. In contrast to mainstream – or at least moderate – religions, however, sport has little tradition of scrutinising its myths, or critiquing its underlying assumptions. In fact, compared to the most prominent churches of the Western world, sport has a woeful record of self-examination, let alone self-criticism.

Sure, there's no end of sporting pundits willing to question everything from football refereeing decisions to the legality of certain cricket bowling actions. But where is the evidence of deeper reflection?

Sport has largely been left in the hands of people who proudly call themselves fanatics. Intellectuals are loath to debate the subject, because if they criticise sport they leave themselves open to the charge of elitism (a crime that today roughly equates to witchcraft in the Middle Ages), and if they praise it they are almost sure to attract scorn from their bookish peers. To professional philosophers, and especially those who write hifalutin newspaper opinion pieces, sport is not *serious*; it is a matter to be addressed only in a detached, mocking tone. But the fact is that sport is quite serious to Pat, the Manchester United fan, and to millions like him.

It's also quite serious to me. I have, I must admit, invested a large part of my life in sport. I've played – with enthusiasm rarely matching skill – games from cricket to golf, and football to squash. I've spent some of my formative years in dimly-lit snooker halls, and some of my happiest ones on a river rowing for my college team. I retain sporting mementoes that mark out the chapters of my life better than any biography could – from a school Sports Day relay medal (courtesy of a courageous last leg in the 4×50 metres) to a shiny brass plaque for once completing the marathon; from countless match-day ticket stubs, to a string of autographs from the days when I was into fast cars, including one signature of the late Ayrton Senna – procured while he was racing in Formula 3 as mere Ayrton de Sylva.

There scarcely seems to be an event of significance in my life that wasn't somehow related to sport. The first time I left home for any length of time was for a three-day tennis tournament in the west of Ireland. It was at the same event that I first kissed a girl.

My first holiday with a girlfriend was a camping trip to the Cheltenham Festival in the Cotswolds. Some years later, we were married and went on honeymoon to Rome, which was best remembered (by me, anyway) for a Lazio game that we managed to take in at the Stadio Olimpico (yes, she is very understanding). My first venture in journalism was as a horseracing columnist in a local newspaper. Today, and even at this very moment, I'm fighting an urge to log on to the internet and check out the latest West Ham team transfer gossip.

This book tries to explain my obsession – an obsession, I know, that is shared by many others. In writing it, I have sought guidance from existing research in psychology, medicine, social science, and other relevant disciplines. Specifically, I have scrutinised much conventional wisdom surrounding sport, and have found that most of what we take to be the Gospel Truth is, in fact, quite the reverse. In considering widely-accepted claims about sport, and especially its supposed positive influence on humankind, one should bear in mind what John Kenneth

Galbraith had to say about common sense. 'To a very large extent,' he wrote, 'we associate truth with convenience – with what most closely accords with self-interest and personal well-being or promises to avoid awkward effort or unwelcome dislocation of life.'

I must admit, by writing this book my relationship with sport has changed – for I reach conclusions which run contrary to my initial thinking; to the thinking on which I was bred, or, dare I say, indoctrinated. If you believe that reflecting in a critical fashion on sport will spoil your enjoyment of it, you are probably right. Anyone who doesn't want their fantasy world interfered with should, therefore, leave the proverbial lecture room now. But take heed of Roger Bannister's warning. Adapting a famous quote of Socrates, Sir Roger – who confessed to be prouder of his life's work as a neurologist than of his record-breaking sub-four-minute mile – once said: 'The unexamined sporting life is not worth living.'

CHAPTER 1

HEADERS AND HEADCASES:
SPORT AND STUPIDITY

'England have the best fans in the world and Scotland's fans are second-to-none'
former England player and manager, Kevin Keegan

'Being thick isn't an affliction if you're a footballer'
Brian Clough, ex-manager, Nottingham Forest

'Thus so wretched is man … and so frivolous is he that, though full of a thousand reasons for weariness, the least thing, such as playing billiards or hitting a ball, is sufficient enough to amuse him'
Blaise Pascal, scientist

A necdotes are a dangerous thing. One swallow does not make a summer. And two swallows is not a trend, no matter what some lazy sports hack will tell you. Wayne Rooney might have a short fuse but that doesn't mean young footballers are petulant. Zinedine Zidane performed the world's best step-over and Thierry Henry exudes a certain *va-va-voom* but they alone don't prove the existence of Gallic flair.

Having said all that, some anecdotes are difficult to ignore, especially if they emerge over time in such a consistent and unwavering pattern as the following:

'I've had 14 bookings this season – 8 of which were my fault, but 7 of which were disputable' – Paul Gascoigne

Or:

'If we start counting our chickens before they hatch, they won't lay any eggs in the basket' – Bobby Robson

Or:

'I've had an interest in racing all my life, or longer really' – Kevin Keegan

Many people, chief among them lazy sports hacks, conclude from such utterances that footballers, as well as football managers (who tend to be ex-footballers), are stupid. The image of the brainless soccer zillionaire, devoid of taste and flapping around a dim-witted dolly-bird, is particularly ingrained in the public psyche. But it's a false impression. As former Hertha Berlin coach, Hans Meyer, once pointed out, you get all types in football. 'From a 25-man squad, two would be able to complete a university degree, and five to six would finish college,' he said. 'Around 12 would make a good living doing skilled manual labour or working as a bank clerk, but certainly five are completely stupid ... and at least one of those would end up begging on the streets if he didn't play pro-fessional football … This is the same for every team.'

According to Meyer's estimate, the proportion of play-ers falling into the 'completely stupid' category appears high. But would the break-down be any different in other occupations, sports journalism included? Comparative IQ tests suggest that athletes receive an unjustified bad press in this area. In one study in the United States, American football players scored a little worse than both bank tell-ers and newswriters, and marginally better than security guards. The differences were so slight across the four categories, however, as to be virtually immaterial. There is little research elsewhere indicating that footballers, or other athletes, are stupid *per se*. But what we can say with some certainty is that people behave stupidly when they play, watch, or otherwise engage in sport.

• SPORT IS KIND OF DUMB •

Consider boxing. No, too obvious.

Consider rugby. Why would anyone in his, or her, right mind actually play rugby? Even if every game was a clean one – devoid of eye-gouging, stamping, spear-tackling, head-butting, or punching – you are unlikely to escape without debilitating injury, especially if your career in the game is a long one. Broken bones, banjaxed knees and the threat of a neck-break or serious head injury are part and parcel of the sport. And what do you get in return? Glory? Exercise? A 'character-building' experience? Even if these were justifiable goals, there are safer ways of achieving them.

In fairness to people who engage in hazardous sports, they are perfectly aware that they are behaving stupidly. Rugby players, jockeys, and so on, universally admit that they would not do what they do if they thought about the risks. Blocking out reasoned argument is a part of competing. As Ellen MacArthur, the death-defying, record-breaking yachtswoman, once said: 'You don't think about death. If you go out there thinking you won't come back, you'll not bother setting out.' Logic deems that one shouldn't risk one's life for a boat race. But MacArthur doesn't listen to logic, and that's exactly what makes her an elite sportswoman. Her sporting success depends upon a lack of reason; a willingness to not think but instead 'just do it'.

It's fair to say that the riskier the pursuit the more consciously stupid it is. Note how so-called adrenaline junkies engaged in stunt-riding and other such 'X-treme' sports proudly describe one another as 'insane'. Sport at this level of risk cannot be logically justified. Buttboarding champion Darren Lott once proved the point when he wrote about his chosen pursuit, which involves propelling oneself, while lying flat on a skateboard, down steep hills that are populated by moving motor cars and other such hazards. Lott himself set a 'street-luge' record of 65.24 miles per hour on a residential road in Arizona in September 1998. (Butt pilots – as they prefer to be known – do keep records, amazingly. The pursuit's governing body is the pompous-sounding International Gravity Sports Association.) In his autobiography, Lott said he loved 'riding on the edge'. But wasn't buttboarding unreasonably dangerous? 'There are plenty of other more efficient ways to get killed or arrested,' the Californian replied.

It is perhaps easy to ridicule surfing-dude types like Lott. But do participants in other sporting codes think any clearer about the risks associated with their games? In 1881, a self-proclaimed 'old football captain' wrote a letter to an Irish sports magazine, expressing contempt for people who had depicted competitive games as hazardous. The correspondent explained that he had once almost been killed by a horse and carriage while crossing the road but that he was saved by 'an old football dodge'. 'I am perfectly certain that football saved my life,' he concluded, displaying a sense of logic no less fuzzy than Lott's. A lifetime of kicks-on-the-shins might well have helped the 'old football captain' to be particularly quick on his feet. But a lifetime of ballet, or ballroom dancing, would surely have also done the trick. And what was the bloke doing standing in the middle of the road in the first place? One blow on the head too many from his playing days, perhaps?

Of course, the fact that sport is inherently risky doesn't make it stupid. Sport is stupid only in instances where the risk of participation disproportionately outweighs potential returns. But what are the returns of sport? If sporting evangelists can be believed, competitive game-playing makes you not only healthy but also wealthy and wise.

Such evangelists are, in every sense, selling us a lie.

• SPORTS FANS ARE POOR RISK-ASSESSORS •

Taking the question of sport's impact on personal health first, few athletes are fully cognisant of the risks associated with their games. Fewer still are cognisant of the risks relative to other sporting pursuits, let alone to non-sporting pursuits, that potentially provide similar benefits.

Ask yourself: What is the most dangerous sport for women athletes in America? Wrestling? Ice-skating? Cycling? Try 'cheerleading'. Recent research shows the injury rate in the 'sport' – which in a college setting in the US closely resembles high-wire acrobatics – is responsible for a higher number of serious injuries, including paralysis, than any other sport. Moreover, the rate of injury in the discipline is increasing rapidly, with one study reporting that there were nearly six times as many emergency room visits for cheerleaders in 2004 as in 1980. Jessica Smith, an eighteen-year-old cheerleader at Sacramento City College, told the *New York Times* in March 2007: 'They make you sign a medical release when you join a cheerleading team. They ought to tell the girls that they are signing a death waiver.' Smith broke her neck in two places when a botched stunt dropped her head-first from a height of about fifteen feet.

Other research has thrown up similarly surprising findings. A study in New Zealand once found that gymnasts suffered a higher rate of injury than rugby players. In New Zealand! A country where rugby is played with unparalleled ferocity.

It would be facetious to argue that exercise is bad for your health. But the benefits of such activity, both physically – in terms of counteracting heart disease, for one – and mentally – in terms of stimulating 'feel good' endorphins in the brain – must be weighed against the disadvantages. There are visible downsides to exercise – injury, and the occasional heart attack among Sunday joggers, for example – and there are invisible ones. Dr Derren Ready, a clinical microbiologist at University College Hospital, London, has studied the latter in great detail, looking specifically at bacteria which breed on equipment that is typically used by 'keep fit' fans. In a somewhat gruesome study, he took swabs from different exercise mats at a London gym and discovered that one location harboured as many as 132 million bugs in an area the size of a 2p coin. The average count for the same area across all the equipment was 16 million bugs. Dr Ready pointed out that this compared to the mere 500 bugs you would expect to find in a 2p-sized area on a toilet seat.

It's worth noting, moreover, that the benefits of exercise can be gained without ever forking out a few hundred pounds a year to sit on someone else's sweat, let alone shelling out a multiple of that to join some golf or tennis club. 'We are not in trouble because people aren't going to the gym and playing sport,' says Professor Ken Fox of Bristol University's exercise and health sciences department. 'The reason we're in trouble is we've stopped being active in our general routines … Raking leaves, Hoovering, even climbing the stairs, are all good forms of moderate exercise.'

The key question here, then, is not 'What health benefits does sport provide?' But, rather, 'What health benefits does sport provide over and above Hoovering?'

The truth is that sport exacts a heavy toll on public finances through injuries and related lost work hours. Sports injuries comprise about one-third of all injuries reported to medical agencies in the UK. Soccer alone is estimated to cost the British taxpayer about £1 billion each year through direct treatment costs and indirect loss of production from the resultant problem of 'time off work'. An estimated 750,000 people report to the casualty wards of British hospitals each year seeking treatment for injuries incurred while playing games or exercising. Just how many of these were trying to imitate the somersaulting celebrations of certain Premier League football stars is anyone's guess. But there's no doubt many amateur athletes simply don't know what they are doing to their bodies when they participate in sport.

Not that we should live our lives wrapped in cotton wool. It's important, as children especially, to engage in activities that help to teach us about physical courage, endurance and dexterity – a point acknowledged even by the Royal Society for the Prevention of Accidents. 'We need to ask ourselves whether it is better for a child to break a wrist falling out of a tree, or to get a repetitive strain wrist injury at a young age from using a computer or video games console,' said the society's leisure safety chief Peter Cornall. 'We believe that children can learn valuable lifelong lessons, particularly about risks and how to deal with them, from playing in the natural environment … Bumps, bruises and grazes are not serious injuries and are part of growing up.'

Outdoorsy rough-and-tumble is one thing, however. Sport – with its propensity for dangerous excess – is another. There's something about sport which drives people to surrender all concern for their personal welfare. I recall, for example, having a kick-around with some friends during a World Cup summer some years ago, when one of our party decided to attempt a Peter Crouch-like bicycle kick. Predictably, he was taken to hospital with a dislocated shoulder. I myself was once stupid enough to take up long-distance running without engaging in the slightest bit of preparation, or research. I was eighteen miles into a practice jog for the marathon when it struck me: I probably should have consumed some water en route. Luckily, I didn't collapse in a dehydrated state. But others have paid dear for similar ignorance – ignorance that is specifically generated by spectator sport, and the cavalier 'I can do that' attitude that it inspires in couch potatoes.

Sport may well have a role in combating obesity in society. But, ironically, it may also be contributing to it. The problem with sport is that – unlike free play, or indeed Hoovering – it is inherently tied up with winning and losing, and also with 'quality control'. It's common practice in schools today to segregate the athletically gifted from those less gifted, and to effectively discourage the latter from further participation in games that will – it is assumed – only cause them embarrassment. The legacy of such 'investment' in sport can perhaps be seen in the growing number of children who have been turned off exercise altogether.

In the US, some educators are questioning whether competitive sports are actually *contributing* to the country's fattening. They argue that an over-emphasis on winning is not just running bookish types off the playing fields but also creating widespread premature 'burnout' in gifted athletes.

As for sport supposedly generating wealth, one of the many sporting lies told in the US is that games like basketball and American football provide young, disadvantaged youths a 'ticket out of the ghetto'. In truth, sport is an incredibly dumb career move. Studies show that less than 1 per cent of collegiate athletes go on to make a living out of sport. For the 99 per cent who fail to make the grade, there are very limited options for employment. A recent survey of athletes in top US sporting colleges showed that those involved in the most competitive games performed worst in exams. While 60 per cent of all athletes graduated in six years, the figure dropped to 35 per cent for basketball players. Noting how the collegiate system produces what he calls 'educational cripples', African American author Earl Ofari Hutchinson has written critically of the black population's 'obsession' with sport in the US. 'The sports delusion among many young blacks blurs the line between reality and fantasy,' he says. 'Coaches know this better than anyone does. They wheel and deal to ram as many blacks as they can into their school's uniforms. The name of the game is not study, baby, study; but win, baby, win.'

Sport may well have a role to play in education – by complementing so-called 'academic' disciplines. But substituting sport for education is almost certainly a road to ruin. Ai Dongmei, a Chinese former champion marathon runner, will – among others – vouch for this. Ai made headlines in China in 2007 when she put her medals up for sale, having been reduced to hawking popcorn and children's clothes on a street corner to make a living. 'I regret bringing her into this sport,' her uncle said at the time. 'If she hadn't become a runner, she might have gone to school and learned something useful to support herself.'

Sports enthusiasts tend to brush over such stories, concentrating instead on the isolated tales of people seemingly escaping poverty, or otherwise improving themselves materially, through sport. One such person is

Manchester United star Cristiano Ronaldo, who remarked after picking up a string of awards in 2007: 'My fifth grade teacher would be surprised to see me now: whenever I came to class, sometimes late, always with the ball in one hand, she would admonish me: "Ronaldo, forget the ball. The ball will not feed you. Do not miss classes. School is what really matters, not the ball. That will not bring you anything in life."' Ronaldo's delight at choosing the sporting life over the scholarly one was qualified, however. In the same interview, he said: 'I am sorry I did not study more, but I had to make my choice in life … To study and to play football at the same time was not compatible and I started to slowly realise that.'

There are similar riders attached to sample cases of athletes transferring victories on the pitch to success in fields like business and politics. Take, for example, the Legend of Richard Branson. We are told – in his autobiography, and elsewhere – that, despite being a poor scholar, Branson captained his local school football team with honour. But does that mean every sporty but academically ungifted adolescent will grow up to be an entrepreneurial whiz?

One piece of research that sheds some light on the issue was conducted in 2005 by Mori. The polling company surveyed 105 'captains of industry' in the UK and reported that almost exactly half captained a sports team in school. Naturally, some of the respondents could have lied – it's not unknown for public individuals to overstate their successes as youths. But, even if the responses were true, one can only conclude from the survey that leadership skills may be developed at a young age. Mori was understandably silent on whether there was a specific link between participation in sport and success in the corporate world. To comment on the matter with any credibility, it would have to have studied what exactly happened to all those ex-players and ex-captains who didn't make it 'big' after school.

But even if a link could be established between sports participation in youth and business success in adulthood, the question remains: Do we want to produce a world of Richard Bransons? One wonders, for example, how many top scientists, or university professors, excelled at sport in school. One also wonders how many political leaders were genuinely athletic as youngsters (as opposed to being retrospectively so, courtesy of some sexed-up curriculum vitaes). Nelson Mandela is one example of a genuine ex-sporting statesman. He was an avid boxer. But, then, so too was the Ugandan despot and so-called 'Last King of Scotland', Idi Amin.

Incidentally, Mandela conducted a little survey of his own – that has parallels to the Mori poll – on entering Johannesburg prison for the first time as a young man. He recalled, in a bitter-sweet episode, that 'almost the entire executive leadership' of the anti-apartheid struggle – 105 Africans, 21 Indians, 23 Whites and seven 'Coloureds' – had been forced to strip naked and line up against a wall. 'Despite my anger, I could not suppress a laugh as I scrutinised the men around me,' he later wrote in his autobiography. 'If fine bodies and impressive physiques were essential to being a leader, I saw that few among us would have qualified.'

As for sport 'making you wise', the evidence is quite the reverse. Various pieces of research suggest that participation in competitive games is detrimental to cognitive and academic functioning. A 2007 study in South Africa found that boys who participated in schools rugby suffered intellectually, mainly – it was postulated – as a result of repeated concussions. A total of 150 'high functioning' pupils from privileged socio-economic status were tested over three years for the report. The performance of rugby players in abstract thinking tests fell over that period, while the performance of students who didn't play the sport rose. Researcher Debra Alexander, a senior clinical psychologist, said mild concussions in rugby 'are too often just dismissed,' noting 'at this stage of their lives the boys' brains are at a critical stage of development.'

A more contentious question is whether heading a ball in soccer contributes to brain damage. There have been calls in the US for compulsory headgear in the sport after researchers discovered that close to 29,000 girls and 21,000 boys in American high school soccer teams suffer concussions each year. (Explaining the difference between genders, the authors cited a possible under-reporting of dizziness and amnesia in 'macho' males. Other researchers have cited the relatively weaker neck muscles of women as a factor.) While the jury is still out on the matter, a precautionary approach is probably justified. Certainly, no one is recommending a return to the heavy leather balls of the early 20th century that, in rain, took on the constitution of solid rock. Another sporting pursuit of which we should be wary is exercising alone – a habit of elite athletes. According to one team of researchers, jogging solo impedes the growth of neurons in the brain, specifically through a lack of social interaction.

As for the impact of sport on the mental health of spectators, on this we can be a good deal more emphatic. Spectator sport has caused what could be labelled a genocide of brain cells, thanks to its close association with alcohol consumption and the allied practice of 'vegging' in front of the television.

Just look at what happens to you when you watch a match. You clear your mind of all concerns. Your critical intellectual faculties shut down. You struggle to communicate with loved ones beyond grunting and shushing at them. You may even start to drool. And, as the exercise is repeated, you begin to embrace the state of mental passivity that sport generates. Your brain feels mushier, your horizons become more limited, and your propensity to perform stupid acts in the name of sport increases. Before you know it, you are empathising with people like the Beijing soccer spectator who raced out of his burning home during a 2006 World Cup match, clutching his television set in his arms, and leaving his wife and child behind to fend for themselves. (Incidentally, the man didn't stop there. His wife recalled: 'After getting out of the house, he then set about finding an electric socket to plug in and continue watching his game.')

For many spectators, the very appeal of sport is its stupefying effect. After a hard day's work, a football fan likes nothing better than to 'switch off' in front of a televised game. This and similar practices may be pleasurable but they are also a type of cognitive cop-out, or a means of problem-avoidance. This, at least, has been my own experience. In school, for example, I used to develop an all-consuming interest in Test cricket precisely at exam-time. The obsession would make studying near-impossible (I mean, you could hardly be expected to abandon a game mid-innings) and, tellingly, my interest in cricket would completely disappear as soon as the exams were over. There is little research in this area, but it's hard to see how regular sports viewing wouldn't impair human intelligence. Men are often accused of not being able to concentrate on two things at once. Is it any wonder when they spend so much of their lives in front of TV screens, focusing intently on a small ball ping-ponging about the place?

Here we touch upon an undeniable truth:

• **THE SPORTIEST SOCIETIES ARE ALSO THE DUMBEST** •
One word for you: Australia.

Another word for you: Brazil. The South American state may be good at football, but its education standards are shockingly low. In a comprehensive survey of international reading habits, Brazil ranked 27th out of 30 countries, with the average Brazilian reading 1.8 non-academic books a year – less than half the figure for Europe and the United States.

It so happens a group of citizens in one Brazilian city unsuccessfully attempted to highlight this literacy problem at the last Fifa World Cup. The three men stripped naked and walked around the city's streets during Brazil's match against Ghana, protesting at the manner in which 'the whole country stops to watch the football matches during the World Cup, while enormous problems in Brazil – like a lack of education among many people … – keep getting worse'. Needless to say, the trio was proverbially pissing in the wind. The protest went unwitnessed by the media and unnoticed by pretty much everyone else. 'Someone called us to check this out,' a police spokesman said of the demonstration. 'But it was not a violent crime and we were watching the match so we decided not to do anything about it.'

In truth, education and sport are far from complementary disciplines. A tension exists between the two realms of discovery that mimics the never-ending friction between science and religion. Like physicists and creationists who loathe each other's company, geeks and jocks occupy opposite ends of a social and intellectual spectrum. Some geeks perhaps wouldn't mind being jocks, or at least having some jock-like qualities. But jocks abhor everything geeks stand for. A jock who admits to reading the *Guardian* or watching BBC's *Newsnight Review* runs the risk of censure or ridicule. Just ask ex-Chelsea footballer Graeme le Saux, who was labelled 'gay' by elements within soccer after he admitted to enjoying opera. Or ask Pat McInally, an American football player, who once scored perfect marks in an IQ test carried out annually on NFL players. 'I was ostracised,' said the Harvard graduate and former Cincinnati Bengals punter. 'There were some awkward moments when I boarded the team plane with a hardcover book under my arm.'

The most insidious thing about this culture of anti-intellectualism is the way in which it can dumb-down the brightest of people. Sport provides an outlet for acceptance, and it's tempting for clever but socially inept individuals to embrace the pursuit as some sort of route to fulfilment. The following dynamic is commonplace:

The geek looks with envy at the jock, at the jock's girlfriends, at the jock's mates, at the way the jock is so goddamn passionate about such a seeming irrelevance as sport, and the geek says to himself: 'I want a bit of that.' For the geek, sport becomes a delicious indulgence, a gateway to the forbidden world of the pack. The geek follows 'his' club. He brushes up on its history, and can rattle off its goal-scoring statistics better than any jock. He subscribes to the club's fanzine, and contributes to supporters' internet chat-sites. He buys lots of stuff from the merchandise shop on match day. In the grandstand he jabs his finger in the air, and joins jocks and fellow geeks in chanting at the opposition, 'You're s**t and you know you are.' When a goal is scored the geek is embraced by a tattooed thug next to him who has been spouting racial abuse since kick-off. The geek hugs the jock-like beast, and enjoys the guilty pleasure. At last, he feels accepted. But accepted into what?

The sorry decline into gang culture appears to be particularly pronounced in Britain, where taking no interest in football is a sure way of being bullied in school, and ignored in adulthood. Longing to be accepted by others, people of a geekish disposition adopt a false accent, downplay their education, and eradicate other signs of 'poshness' (hey, I've done it myself on occasion). For many a geek, the role model is author Nick Hornby, a graduate of English Literature at Cambridge University, and son of millionaire businessman Sir Derek Hornby. In *Fever Pitch*, and other works, Hornby reveals his long-time support of Arsenal Football Club, and in doing so articulates how someone from a privileged middle-class background can develop the aura, if not the identity, of a downtrodden working-class hero. The secret is not necessarily to be 'one of them' but to avoid being 'one of us', as Hornby suggests in the following passage:

> In 1990, when England played Cameroon in the quarterfinals of the World Cup, it wasn't hard to find people in England – middle-class, liberal people, admittedly, but people nonetheless – who wanted Cameroon to win. I watched that game with some of them, and when England went 2–1 down (they eventually won 3–2 in extra time), these people cheered. I understood why, but I couldn't cheer with them, much to my surprise. Those drunk, racist thugs draped in the national colours … They were, it turned out, my people, not the nice liberal friends I was watching the game with …

Whether Hornby will ever be accepted by the 'drunk, racist thugs' to whom he purportedly relates is somewhat debatable. What is certain, however, is that his chances of social inclusion rise each time he trash-talks 'nice' middle-class liberals.

In fairness to Hornby, he has never tried to disguise the irrational nature of his footballing passion. In *Fever Pitch*, he described it with admirable candour as 'lunacy'. Labelling football as 'the great retardant', he explained how 'the light of intelligence' departed him after his team won an unlikely league title in 1988–89. When it comes to football, 'I rarely *think*,' he wrote. 'I remember, I fantasise, I try to visualise every one of Alan Smith's goals, I tick off

the number of First Division grounds I have visited …
None of this is *thought*, in the proper sense of the word.
There is no analysis, or self-awareness, or mental rigour
going on at all, because obsessives are denied any kind of
perspective on their own passion.'

In this manner, Hornby is the authentic voice of the
fan. After all:

• FANS THRIVE ON BEHAVING STUPIDLY •

A simple test for the above. Of the following pair, which
is the real sports fan?

*(1) Dave supports Liverpool. He watches them on TV as
often as he can, and once or twice a year he goes to Anfield
for a match. He would like to go more often, but since the
twins were born he finds he has less time. His wife, Jane, has
a demanding job, and she likes to unwind at weekends by
walking in the countryside with her family. On such out-
ings, Dave sometimes carries a portable radio with him so
he can keep track of match-day scores. When Liverpool win,
Dave makes a mental note of the team's progress. When they
lose, he is disappointed but he gets on with life. Dave speaks
of his wedding day as the happiest day of his life, and the
twins' birthday the next happiest. A 'close third', he says,
was Liverpool's victory in the Champions League in 2005.
The day after the final, he wore into work a necktie with
'You'll Never Walk Alone' printed on it. Jane had bought it
for him a few years previously as a Christmas present.*

(2) Mike supports Manchester United. A season ticket-holder at Old Trafford, he never misses a home game and travels to every second away fixture. Occasionally he will attend a family function on match day, but only when United are playing somewhere like Craven Cottage and there's no live coverage on Sky Sports. Mike renewed his season ticket this year despite claims from his wife, Alison, that money was tight, what with the recent arrival of Alex and Waynella. The twins are doing fine, although Alison wasn't too impressed by Mike's disappearance during the Caesarean to catch the second half of Everton vs. Man Utd in a pub across the road from the maternity hospital.

Mike recently got a tattoo across his shoulder blades reading 'United until I die'. He had already got one on his left arm that said 'Wes Brown'. Last year, Mike and Alison renewed their wedding vows at a special pitch-side ceremony during half-time of Man Utd vs. Portsmouth. When United win, Mike talks boastfully about them being 'Champions of Europe'. When they lose, Mike curses a lot and goes into a grump. He suffered a mini-heart attack during the closing stages of the 1999 Champions League Final. The following day, he marched into work and painted the slogan 'Treble-winners' in Tipp-Ex on a computer screen belonging to his colleague Dave, a Liverpool fan.

Being a genuine sports fan requires ever-increasing displays of stupidity. The dumber you behave, the more your currency rises as a supporter.

Sport's relationship with stupidity doesn't end there, though. Leave fans to one side and consider again just what it is that defines sport. All sport involves risk but also, on some level, brawn. A pursuit that is not, in some way, physical cannot be classified as sport. Thus, athletics, which tests bodily strength and agility, is sport. Darts and snooker, which test eye–hand coordination, are sport. But chess is not sport. And nor indeed are card games – any more than sitting around sipping brandies and discussing world affairs can be called sport (sorry to break it to you, members of the toastmasters' club, you are *not* the debating equivalents of the Galacticos). Obviously, sportspeople do have functioning brains. But to describe their defining skill as 'intelligence' is a corruption of language. A more accurate label is kinesthetic ability – an uncanny awareness of one's bodily position, weight or movement.

American author David Foster Wallace explains this ability with reference to Roger Federer, a tennis sensation who can swat away 150mph service balls as though they were sluggish flies. 'For promising junior players, refining the kinesthetic sense is the main goal of the extreme daily practice regimens we often hear about,' Foster Wallace writes. 'Hitting thousands of strokes, day after day, develops the ability to do by "feel" what cannot be done by regular conscious thought … So one type of technical explanation for Federer's dominion is that he's just a bit more kinesthetically talented than the other male pros. Only a little bit, since everyone in the top 100 is himself kinesthetically gifted – but then, tennis is a game of inches.'

Foster Wallace describes the kinesthetic sense as 'both muscular and neurological' but whatever it is, it is not intellectual. After all, it is a *sense* – a kind of feeling rather than reasoning. The kinesthetic sense is, moreover, not unique to athletes – something of which the sporting world appears to be blissfully unaware. Tradesmen, medics, and various other professionals who work with their hands, have also developed high standards of kinesthetic ability – but you wouldn't think so, listening to sports commentators waffling on about the peculiar 'genius' of tennis or football players. If Ronaldinho deserves to be praised for his 'vision' when completing a pass, then surely the average chef does too when standing over an erect soufflé. (A little exercise in the spirit of helping to generate parity: Next time you eat out in a restaurant, greet every action of your waiter with a toady sigh and an exclamation along the lines of 'Olé!' or 'Maestro!' On exit, pay tribute to his 'waitering brain'.)

The truth is that sport has appropriated the language of intelligence to cover up for its brainless qualities. Note, for example, how soccer players and coaches are routinely given the honorary title of 'The Professor'. Bizarrely, not one but two members of the French squad bore this moniker in the sporting press during the 2006 Fifa World Cup. One was the captain, Zinedine Zidane, whose final act in the tournament was to head-butt an opponent.

The other was the coach, Raymond Domenech, who consulted astrologers when making his team selections (dropping Robert Pires because he fell under the star sign of Scorpio).

Not surprisingly, professional commentators seem particularly eager to promote sport as an intellectual enterprise. These people used to be called 'match announcers' in days of yore. Now they are called 'analysts', and theirs is a licence to talk nonsense. In fact, no analyst today worth his salt (and it is still generally 'his' salt) will limit his comments to match tactics, something on which he might well have an informed view. The contemporary analyst will have an 'expert opinion' on players' mental and emotional states, on the moral import of particular sporting incidents, and – if David Beckham is playing – on the latest trends in gents' hairdressing. This penchant for empty pontificating can be seen each Saturday in newspaper opinion columns – columns which read something like a *Father Ted* sermon.

'Life (or football) is not meant to be fair … Or perhaps it is … Or perhaps it's not … Or perhaps it is … Is my five minutes up yet?'

That sort of thing.

Arguably, soccer analysis reached its nadir with Zidane's sending-off in Berlin in 2006. Such was the unexpected nature of the event, pundits lost all control of their faculties, producing such prose as the following:

Had the tensions between the real Zidane and the Zidane of fantasy become too much? One certainty: reality was no longer measuring up to Zidane's perception of the way life should be. That headbutt was not a rational act. Nor did it represent a mere Rooney moment – a flash of violent temper aimed at someone who had annoyed him. Rather, it was an act of cosmic discontent. It was a futile gesture of protest against the cruelties of sport and the far greater cruelties of time … In his last match, it was the belief that he [Zidane] was above the reach of normal men that brought him down.

This was part of an article which ran in *The Times* under the heading 'How Zidane's Belief Brought Him Down'. As a representation of sports analysis today, it is perhaps the best argument you could come up with to scrap such commentary from newspapers, or at least move it onto the same page as the horoscopes and the funnies.

Ironically, 'opinion' such as that above will guarantee you a long career in sporting punditry, whereas stating the obvious, or even the factually accurate, will lead to ridicule – and over time, probably the sack. Witness how commentators are lampooned for making statements like: 'Well, either side could win it, or it could be a draw' (ex-pundit Ron Atkinson); or 'Argentina won't be at Euro 2000 because they're from South America' (Kevin Keegan). Such comments may be banal but you can't fault their logic. Once you go beyond stating the scoreline in a sporting contest you are in danger of entering the realm of fantasy, or embracing hyperbole (which itself is a form of fantasy).

Tolerance for logic is especially thin on the ground in television – and understandably so, given the medium's obsession with 'performance'. Some of the blame for this goes back to Jimmy Hill, the ex-Fulham player, who as head of ITV sport in 1970 introduced what was then the UK's first 'expert panel' for a Fifa World Cup. 'I wanted men conceited enough to think that their opinion was the right one,' Hill said of the initiative. The demands of television punditry are unchanged today. The most sought-after commentators are not the most coherent but the most entertaining. Lateral thinkers like Alan Shearer ('You only get one opportunity of an England debut') are tolerated but only if they have some other cachet, like Shearer does as an iconic former England captain. This cachet doesn't always last, however. Even Dutch footballing superstar Johan Cruyff found TV jobs drying up in the Netherlands after he gained a reputation for 'Cruyffisms' such as 'If we have the ball, they can't score', and, 'It doesn't matter if the opposing side scores a goal as long as you score one more than them'.

Rather than inspiring mirth, ex-footballers who try to make it as TV pundits surely deserve some sympathy. People laugh at them for, say, mixing up their metaphors but you can see how easily that could happen. Their task, after all, is to try to intellectualise the unintelligent; to make the shallow seem more interesting. Thus, a pundit who wants to say that his team is doing well can't, for example, comment: 'My team is doing well.' No, he must embellish the most straightforward of statements, *especially* the most straightforward of statements. He must also avoid repeating himself – a difficult task, given the limited vocabulary he can call upon to describe some men kicking a ball around a field. A typical piece of commentary might see the pundit set off with a particular metaphor in mind, only to realise mid-stream that he has being using it a bit too often. Evasive action is taken, and you end up with such 'analysis' as the following: 'The tide is very much in our court now' (Kevin Keegan), or 'We all know that promotion is the carrot at the end of the tunnel' (Mark Yardley).

The attempts of professional commentators to 'brain-up' sport are daft enough, but more hilarious still are the like-minded efforts of academics. Being a huge and ever-growing industry, sport is an attractive study topic for social scientists, philosophers and other such 'cultural' interpreters. Yet among the thousands of sports-related articles clogging up humanities departments across the globe, has a single piece of research ever done anything other than either: (a) state the bleedin' obvious, or (b) get lost up a hole of its own creation?

An example of the former comes from psychologist Dr Cathy Craig of Queen's University Belfast, who recruited a research team to study the psychological forces at play in free-kick situations on the soccer pitch. Intrigued by a spectacular Roberto Carlos goal in 1997, the researchers studied the reactions of both goalkeepers and outfield players to stationary balls which had been powerfully struck with side-spin. In 'Judging Where a Ball Will Go: the Case of Curved Free Kicks in Football' (2006), Craig C.M. *et al.* identify 'perceptual effects [which] find their origin in inherent limitations of the human visual system in anticipating the arrival point of an object subjected to an additional accelerative influence'. They continue: 'The depth of experience of our participants does not seem to be able to compensate for these shortcomings in visual perception.'

In short, people seem to have difficulty following the trajectory of a spinning ball. Well, like, duh!

And what of the other, let's call it 'abstruse', extreme of sporting research? Well consider this input from Russell Gough, Professor of Philosophy and Ethics at Pepperdine University, California, USA. In 'Moral Development Research in Sports and Objectivity' (1998), he writes (in a parting commentary):

> Concluding that 'the sport structure functions to diminish athletes' sense of moral engagement by concentrating responsibility in the roles of coaches and officials and by codifying appropriate behavior in the form of rules' or that 'participation in

collegiate (but not high school) basketball is associated with lower level moral reasoning in both sport and life' might be construed as personal moral judgments passed on athletes by means of a predetermining, ineliminable *a priori* criterion of moral truth according to which athletes are deemed more or less morally mature to the extent that they compete and generally conduct themselves in the manner of enlightened, liberalist democrats.

Proof, if it was ever needed, that:

● **ALL ATTEMPTS TO INTELLECTUALISE SPORT ARE DESTINED TO FAIL BECAUSE SPORT IS KIND OF DUMB** ●

To digress for a moment, there is a case to be made for an 'artistic' form of sports commentary. Specifically, it might be welcome if sports analysts played a role akin to art critics, in the sense of scrutinising and exploring the meaning of relevant creative works. However, this would require sport to take on a new identity – the identity of an art form. Accordingly, the rules of the game, and even the question of who won and lost, would matter less than the way in which the game was played. Silverware would no longer be the primary measure of success (after all, we don't judge actors on the basis of whether their characters come out on top, or get killed off, in a particular dramatic work), and popularity would not necessarily be synonymous with quality (again, we don't assume a movie to be good because it attracts a large audience). In fact, we accept that the best films are often found in small art-houses rather than in multiplex cinemas, and likewise – in the 'sport as art' scenario – we might have to acknowledge that the 'best' games are located in an amateur, local setting rather than in a professional stadium. In such a world, analysts could speak without contradiction on the hidden meanings of a game of tennis, or the moral implications of a frame of snooker, because all sport would be (and be understood to be) 'performance art'.

Some people already use artistic terminology to describe sporting skills. However, fans and practitioners of sport regard the practice in which they are involved as somehow superior to, or more significant than, art. Note how soccer commentators often compare their particular fancy to warfare but never compare it to crochet or origami. Orwell's remark that 'serious sport is war minus the shooting' has become a favoured mantra of football analysts, and understandably so, given not only the macho culture at the heart of sport but the fact that what matters most – in the current athletic climate – is the result.

None of this is to say that sport is inherently wrong. There is a place for the dumb, after all. We don't need to be reading advanced physics or listening to Mendelssohn all the time. But let's not pretend that sport is some kind of progressive, evolved, or especially civilised pursuit. If one had to classify it, along with other human activities, sport might well be bracketed, not with literature nor with the 'higher arts', but with MTV's *Jackass*. Like 'Firehose Rodeo' or 'Buttrocket' (the latter of which involves lighting a firecracker above one's lowered trousers), sport engages us at a fairly base intellectual level. Just as Johnny Knoxville sniggers inanely as he sees another backside go up in flames, we watch our games and mumble through popcorn-filled mouths, 'Wow!' or 'Wooah! That's gotta hurt!' In fact, arguably, these two particular phrases, or variations of the same, are about all one can legitimately say by way of sports analysis.

An apologist for sport may reply that we need a 'release' from time to time, and maybe even a little dumbing-down. We need our follies, he might say, and sport is no worse than any other. At the end of the day, he might well say ('at the end of the day' being the sort of phrase he would typically use), sport is a bit of innocent fun.

Sport, innocent? In the next chapter we'll see about that.

CHAPTER 2

THE SCHOOL OF HARD KNOCKS: SPORT, CHARACTER AND MORALS

'Jesus Christ says "turn the other cheek", but Figo is not Jesus Christ.'
> Portuguese manager, 'Big Phil' Scolari, on Luis Figo's head-butting of an opponent in a match against Holland in World Cup 2006

'Obviously, it's hard to fulfil Christian ideals on a rugby pitch. There's gamesmanship and you lose the rag every now and again.'
> Irish rugby international, Andrew Trimble

'I want to kill people. I want to rip their stomachs out and eat their children.'
> former world boxing champ, Mike Tyson

Say something often enough and people will believe you. The earth is flat. Iraq has WMDs. Sport is good for you. Yes, we humans are a gullible bunch. The evidence if anything points to the reverse, yet we continue to believe that sport 'improves' people's character.

Just where the idea came from is a matter of some debate. Plato and Aristotle spoke of the importance of gymnastics in a balanced education. Jean-Jacques Rousseau more explicitly linked regular exercise with ethical behaviour, advising the parents of every young boy to 'give his body constant exercise, make it strong and healthy in order to make him good and wise.' It wasn't until the mid-19th century, however, that the idea of sport as a 'character-building' vehicle really took hold.

This was the era of Queen Victoria. The British Empire was at its height, and public schools across the home nations were embracing the philosophy of 'Muscular Christianity'. The thinking was that sport would not only prepare the next generation of British leaders for the hard knocks of life, but instil in them virtues such as self-discipline, courage and justice. (Britain at this time saw no contradiction in preaching Christianity while committing mass murder in the colonies. So, a theory suggesting that boys could be made better through brutalisation had an instant appeal.)

Muscular Christianity is often credited to Dr Thomas Arnold, headmaster of Rugby School from 1829 to 1842. However, the clergyman who was immortalised in the novel *Tom Brown's Schooldays* can only fairly be blamed for inventing the game to which so many Muscular Christians flocked. Dr Arnold envisaged rugby principally as a diversion for his unruly pupils – as an alternative to, as one author put it, the then favourite pursuit of 'marauding the countryside'. It was Dr Arnold's disciples – and notably his assistant master at Rugby, George E.L. Cotton – who viewed team games as a religious medium. Learn your Latin verbs in the morning and partake in an organised brawl in the afternoon and you will be brought closer to God. Such was his message.

Like Dr Arnold, clergyman Cotton featured in *Tom Brown's Schooldays*, the best-selling novel of Thomas Hughes, a past pupil at Rugby. Published in 1857, the book was hugely successful in popularising Muscular Christianity. Part-drama, part-sermon about the 'noble-ness' of harsh physical activity, it climaxed with the tale of Arthur, a weedy newcomer to Rugby, who was saved from persistent bullying by the hot-headed, brawny Tom. Like some perverse biblical parable, Hughes eschewed the ethic of 'turn the other cheek' for that of 'get your retali-ation in first'.

'Fighting with fists is the natural and English way for English boys to settle their quarrels,' Hughes wrote. 'What substitute for it is there, or ever was there, amongst any nation under the sun? What would you like to see take its place? Learn to box, then, as you learn to play cricket and football.'

Similar pleadings were made in the novels of Charles Kingsley, a friend of Hughes, who viewed games like rugby as an 'antidote to the poison of effeminacy … which was sapping the vitality of the Anglican Church.' Typical of Victorian moralists, Kingsley was obsessed with sex. He loathed the idea of other people having 'it', and in team sports like rugby he believed he had a cure, particularly for what have been described as 'the two unmentionables of the Victorian period: masturbation and homosexuality'. Just why writhing around in mucky shorts with other boys would reduce any teenager's libido is anyone's guess. But the theory was perhaps no less barmy than the belief that sport is a route to moral purity.

Barmy or not, the latter theory became accepted wisdom in no time. One staunch believer in it was Baron Pierre de Coubertin, founder of the modern Olympic Games in 1896, who reportedly 'converted' to Muscular Christianity after reading a French translation of *Tom Brown's Schooldays*. Significantly, de Coubertin designed the Games as a showcase for Christian morality. He took the Olympic motto from the words of a French Dominican preacher, and the Olympic creed from a bishop's sermon. A similar, creative exercise was carried out 30 years later by Jules Rimet. Believing that 'sport – and above all football – would be the means to teach the world's masses to appreciate the Christian virtues of hard work, honesty, obedience to rules, comradeship and fair play', Rimet founded what is now called the Fifa World Cup.

The role of Christian evangelists like Cotton, de Coubertin and Rimet in the development of modern sport can't be overstated. If it wasn't for such idealists, and specifically their belief in the redemptive powers of kicking, running and jumping, etc., the world would be a very different place. Remember that until the Muscular Christians made a connection between, on the one hand, vigorous physical exercise and, on the other, virtue, there were no sporting records, no sportsmen, and no sports to talk of. Until about 150 years ago, games like football and golf were ill-defined outdoor activities akin to rambling and hopscotch. (The first rules of football weren't written until 1863, and of golf until 1897.) Modern sport can, thus, be seen as a moral experiment (and a moral experiment that has gone badly wrong – but we will come to that in a moment).

As well as helping to create more organised games, the Muscular Christians and their disciples succeeded in popularising sport through what today might be described as youth literature. Generations of males grew up on a diet of comics such as *Boy's Own*, *Roy of the Rovers*, *Tiger*, *Hotspur*, *Champion*, and other such works that shamelessly hailed the virtues of a sporting ruck. In his book *On the Corinthian Spirit*, D.J. Taylor reviewed this particular brand of propaganda, citing as a standard example of the genre Herbert Hayens' *Play Up Kings!*, one of Taylor's favourite books as a ten-year-old. The book opened on a station platform with a father seeing his son off to boarding school. 'Now go in and win. Live clean, run straight and play the game,' the father advised. 'And don't whine when you get knocked down. That's my sermon.'

When I read the speech I couldn't help but notice the uncanny resemblance it had to a lecture that was delivered in my presence at a similarly important educative juncture. On my last day of secondary school, I was summoned with other school-leavers to the assembly hall to listen to a departing sermon from our headmaster, a

Catholic priest who had spent the previous six years drilling into us the supposed significance of rugby. 'Lads, life is like a rugby match,' began the sermon, which could well have been written by Dr Arnold himself. 'The ball may bounce for you. Or it mightn't bounce for you ...'

Contemporary sporting evangelists such as my former headmaster may retain a certain Christian flavour. But many do not. Just as Christianity has spawned copycat secular belief-systems, Muscular Christianity has produced 'Godless' imitators. Among the latter was the Sportsmanship Brotherhood, an organisation founded in the US in 1926 by a British sportswriter with the goal of spreading the gospel of competitive game-playing. The *New York Times* endorsed the initiative with a gushing editorial. 'Play the game,' the newspaper said. 'That means truthfulness, courage, Spartan endurance, self-control, self-respect, scorn of luxury, consideration for another's opinions and rights, courtesy, and above all fairness. These are the fruits of the spirit of sportsmanship and in them ... lies the best hope of social well-being.'

The Brotherhood faded away as a distinct organisation within a few years of its inauguration – seemingly because its message had become universally accepted. Since Dr Arnold's day, the public's faith in sport's capacity to transform lives for the better has become ever deeper, stronger and more blind. Today, it's common wisdom that sport brings us closer to God, or to goodness. If only it were true.

• SPORT BRINGS OUT THE WORST IN PEOPLE •

Psychologists don't like to agree with one another, but there's no arguing on this point. Over the past 30 years, athletes of varying ability have been quizzed and tested on their moral reasoning skills, their ability to distinguish between self-interest and particular 'sporting' ideals, and their actual behaviour in morally-challenging scenarios. And all the studies point to the same thing. As one team of boffins puts it: 'A strong body of qualitative and quantitative research exists … supporting [the view] that the longer athletes participate in sport, the more their moral reasoning is affected by the competitive experience. Moreover, athletes' reasoning skills are significantly lower than those of their nonathletic peers. It would appear from the research that sport does not model, challenge, support, or teach the critical reasoning skills paramount to making good moral decisions.'

None of this should surprise us. As said before, research on sport tends to be either humbug or banal. You don't need a PhD in locker-room counselling to recognise the psychological risks associated with competitive game-playing. What is surprising, though, is how the research in this area is generally either ignored or suppressed. It never surfaces in public debates about sport. It is never highlighted by sport's governing bodies (even though they are presumably aware of it). And it is never appreciated by politicians who spend vast sums of public money on competitive sports facilities and training schemes for elite athletes.

What the research does show is that team sports – and particularly those with a contact element – are mostly detrimental to one's moral character. The pack mentality dilutes players' sense of individual moral responsibility – all the more so where influential coaching is involved. Games like football and rugby tend to create an environment where nobody thinks they are responsible for wrong-doing – not unlike war, in that sense. If an atrocity is carried out on the battlefield, the soldiers can't be blamed; they were merely following orders. But, then again, the general can't be blamed either because he didn't actually pull the trigger (even though he may have loaded the gun). It's worth noting that, in search of a scapegoat, people often turn to an overriding – but, in practice, frequently powerless – authority. In warfare, it's usually the United Nations ('It should never have allowed the violence to spiral out of control'). In sport, it tends to be the referee ('He/she should never have allowed the violence to spiral out of control').

The landmark research on morality in sport was done in the mid-1980s by Californian psychologists Brenda Jo Bredemeier and David L. Shields. The husband-and-wife team asked people from various sports, and none, for their response to certain ethical dilemmas. These dilemmas were presented in the form of both sporting and non-sporting stories – such as the tale of a married businessman who was wondering whether to end an exploitative sexual relationship with his young secretary, and the scenario of a footballer who had been told by his coach to deliberately try to maim an opposing player. Each subject was interviewed to establish his or her ability to see different points of view. Interviewees were also tested on whether they were more likely to justify the infliction of violence on others, as well as whether they were capable of seeing beyond their own selfish interests in conflict scenarios.

Bredemeier and Shields concluded – and their findings have been corroborated by countless studies since – that participation in competitive sport created 'lower level moral reasoning in both sport and life'. Naturally, there were variations within the studies. The more competitive the sport, the 'lower' the participants' morals tended to be. Stress, in particular, was said to increase 'the frequency of moral defaults'. Women were less likely to be ethically 'led astray' by sport than men, but such differences were only differences of degree. Sport in general was found to encourage both impure thought and unethical behaviour. As Bredemeier and Shields put it:

> Egocentrism is the hallmark of immature reasoning in everyday life, but the sport realm provides socially legitimated opportunities to suspend the usual requirement that others' interest be given equivalent consideration to those of the self.

Or, as Professor Aidan Moran, a psychologist and occasional mind-coach to professional golfer Padraig Harrington, says: 'It's a fairly mythical idea that sport develops traditional virtues like fair play, social cohesion, and respect for opponents. Even in amateur sports, we can give lots of examples of cheating, distortion of the rules and disrespect.'

• Sport resembles play gone wrong •

It could be argued that most of the benefits of sport are really benefits of play. The latter provides exercise, and a socialising experience, and – when practised a certain way – potentially teaches discipline, courage and invention. What 'play' lacks is a genuinely competitive element. Play can be a contest but not a very serious one, and for this reason many see it as superficial, or lacking in practical value.

Some educators have tried to combine healthy aspects of competition with play through experimental games and activities. In the mid-1970s, for example, a Swiss biologist called Dr Hermann Brandt invented a game called tchoukball (pronounced 'chookball') which sought – in the words of its inventor – to be 'a tool to bring peace between teams'. Tchoukball loosely resembles netball but interceptions are forbidden, and there is no physical contact between players. Played on an indoor court with no goals but two upturned mini-trampolines, against which scores are 'created', the game is specifically designed to avoid the sort of injuries common to basketball or squash. Billed as a 'healthy and ethical sport', it comes with its own moral charter which begins: 'The game excludes any striving after prestige, whether personal or collective.' The charter also stipulates: 'The major concern of each player must be to strive after beauty of play. Universal experience in sport can be resumed by the expression: "Elegant playing attracts elegant playing."'

Despite its lofty ambitions, tchoukball resembles a relatively mainstream sport today. Thirty years on from the game's inception, it's holding ever-more commercialised competitions, including 'beach tchoukball' championships. And a campaign has begun to include the discipline in future Olympics. (How long will it be, one wonders, before the first tchoukball doping scandal?) Conceding that the sport is not entirely injury-free, the world governing body for tchoukball launched an 'injury report database' in 2006. As for the supposed ban on 'striving after prestige', you wouldn't know it was there looking at the way national tchoukball federations use their websites to brag about their respective achievements.

It seems that sport can't be made 'good' by simply changing the parameters by which people compete. Rather, athletes must change themselves. The cliché 'nice guys finish second' seems to have some bearing on reality when one looks at someone like Jimmy White, who has been dubbed 'the People's Champion', in large part because of his humble persona, and whose career is defined by six runner-up finishes in the World Snooker Championships. Or Andy Roddick, who has won humanitarian awards for his charity work and wider plaudits for his on-court behaviour, while holding a disappointing record in tennis Grand Slam singles finals, with just one win in four attempts. Gary O'Toole, a former Irish swimming champion who in the 1990s courageously blew the whistle on sexual abuse in the sport, is perhaps a more clear-cut 'decent sort'. Erudite, principled and a qualified medic to boot, he's the kind of guy you would like competitive sports to produce. Is it just a coincidence that his main achievement was a silver medal in the 1989 European Championships? Asked about his failure to win an Olympic title, he once explained: 'I never actually severed all my safety nets. I took a year off university, but always knew I was going back to medicine … I never put myself in that situation where I risked everything. And the more you risk, the higher the payback.'

• SPORT IS ANTI-FAMILY •

The claim that sport 'improves character' is often tied up with another (bogus) claim – namely, that sport strengthens interpersonal relationships or family bonds. Golfers are particularly guilty of disseminating this myth – by arguing, with a whiff of superiority, that their sport is the only pursuit which a father and son can do together throughout their lives, irrespective of their age. To which one can only say: Pl-ease! What a failure of imagination!

And, anyway, even if a father and a son can periodically hack around a course together, a father and a daughter will be prevented from doing so at certain golf clubs, or at certain times of the week, because of sexist and discriminatory rules that apply in the sport.

Personally, I have many a fond memory of travelling to sporting events with my father, but they were not uniquely the occasion for bonding. In recent years, my father and I have played tennis together (sport), we have gone for swims in the sea together (exercise but not sport), and we have played card games together (neither exercise nor sport). Just which pursuit produced the most teary-eyed 'Dad–Son' moments I couldn't tell you. But, for what it's worth, I got the 'facts of life' talk some years ago while we were on a long, meandering walk together, and *not* during one of our regular tennis games. In fact, it's hard to imagine how he could have worked it into the latter.

Naturally, other people will have different experiences of sport as mediated through family members. The soccer writer David Winner has fond memories of attending football matches as a child with his old man, and, as a result, he says he thinks of the sport as 'a vehicle for love, especially between fathers and sons'. To others, however, soccer may be a vehicle for hate, or indifference. Think of all those children who grow up in Boot Camp conditions under pushy, parental coaches. Or think of those children who are shunted – perhaps against their will – from soccer lessons to tennis lessons, to swimming lessons, or to anything else going, with the sole objective that they stay out from under their parents' feet. In her memoir *Not a Games Person*, Julie Myerson explains exactly how sport foisted on youth can generate unhappy memories. As a sensitive, bookish child, she resented having to make what she calls 'the big and terrifying statement that is competing' – and she surely wasn't alone.

Professor Moran notes that parents sometimes have unrealistic expectations about the value of sport to their children, believing that 'something magical happens in between the time they are dropped off and collected from training'. This perhaps mirrors parental attitudes to education generally, with research showing that fathers in particular tend to opt out of schooling decisions. 'They [fathers] are happy to wax lyrical about football, but are no good at discussing serious problems with their children,' according to one psychological study.

The risk of a father neglecting his child almost inevitably rises with the intensity of his devotion to sport. This raises the question of the 'collateral damage' which is caused by a sporting passion. How many relationships have fallen apart because of a congested match-fixture list? How many children have grown up knowing everything about their father's favourite football team – but nothing about their father? How many marriages have broken down over one too many golf weekends with the lads? One of Ireland's top Gaelic Games players, Dara O Cinneide, won a string of championship medals but, he once confessed, 'I had to put back my marriage three times because of it.'

The penchant among modern sportsmen to bring their children onto the pitch during the presentation of trophies is touching. But it hides the fact that sport is essentially anti-family. Athletes are meant to be committed to their team and training schedule; full stop. A revealing comment came from former Manchester City manager Stuart Pearce after his daughter asked him to sit her fluffy doll, 'Beenie the horse', next to him in the dugout. 'It's difficult to tell a seven-year-old, "This is the Premiership, I'm known as Psycho and I'm a hard man."'

Bill Shankly, the legendary Liverpool FC manager, is famous for saying that football is not a matter of life and death – 'it is much more important than that'. But arguably the remark that said most about him was the following: 'Of course I didn't take my wife to see Rochdale as an anniversary present. It was her birthday. And it wasn't Rochdale, it was Rochdale reserves.' People like Shankly became legends in football exactly because they put everything – family included – behind winning. One of Africa's best-loved players, Jomo 'The Black Prince' Sono, was for years reputed to have abandoned his wife at the altar to help his team recover from a first-half deficit in a local game. According to a revised version of the story (which is only marginally more appealing to feminists), Sono timed the wedding to finish before kick-off so he could listen to it on the radio, and on learning that his team were 2–0 down he rushed to the stadium to score two goals and help his team score another brace.

One might see some progress in Alex Ferguson's decision in August 2007 to stay away from a couple of pre-season friendlies to help his wife pack for a family house move. 'I told Cathy that I had a match tonight, but she wasn't having any of that,' the Manchester United boss confessed. 'She said it was a friendly and that I had to help her.' The incident received widespread coverage but it hardly signalled a change in the prevailing attitude within sport towards 'interfering' family members. Bear in mind, Ferguson was only missing a couple of fixtures against Dunfermline and Glentoran. Hardly the greatest sacrifice in the world. Moreover, a few weeks after the episode, Ferguson's prodigy, Roy Keane, launched a broadside against players' wives having a say in their husband's careers. 'Priorities have changed in footballers and they are being dictated to by their wives,' the Sunderland manager said, after experiencing a frustrating week in the transfer market. 'If a player doesn't want to come to Sunderland then all well and good. But if he decides he doesn't want to come because his wife wants to go shopping in London, then it's a sad state of affairs. It's not a football move, it's a lifestyle move. It tells me the player is weak and his wife runs his life. The idea of women running the show concerns me and worries me, but the players we're talking about are soft.'

In fact, it's hard to think of any profession less family-friendly than football. In what other line of work would you be so vilified for spending time with your kith and kin, as Jurgen Klinsmann was in the run-up to the 2006 Fifa World Cup? For several months before the opening of the competition (in which, incidentally, Klinsmann exceeded all expectations – guiding Germany to a third-place finish), the manager commuted between his home nation and the US, where his wife and kids happened to live. For such impertinence, he was accused of lacking commitment to the job. Franz Beckenbauer, *der Kaiser* of German football, described as 'unforgivable' Klinsmann's failure to attend a run-of-the-mill officials' conference in Germany, three months before the opening of the tournament. The coach had missed the event to attend the first anniversary of the death of his father – a commemoration that he had long-before promised to share with his family.

If competitive sport doesn't split families altogether, then it may poison internal relationships – relationships between husband and wife, parent and child, or perhaps between siblings. A particularly unedifying phenomenon is the pushy, ill-mannered 'Tennis Dad' who has become a cliché through his omnipresence. There's Mary Pierce's father and former coach, Jim Pierce, who famously shouted from the sidelines during a game, 'Mary, kill the bitch!' There's Christophe Fauviau, the father of a rising teenage tennis star in France, who was found guilty in 2006 of drugging 27 opponents, killing one. And then there are the countless dads and mums who, this very day, will be screaming at their children, abusing umpires, and fighting with other kids' parents at your local tennis club.

Sadly, tennis is not alone in producing such ogres. In a major survey of attitudes towards sport in Australia, parents were identified across the board as being the most badly behaved cohort of sporting 'participants'. Athletes and non-athletes, but particularly parents themselves, cited repeated evidence of obnoxious parental shenanigans in schools and colleges. 'One negative behaviour commonly witnessed was parents putting too much pressure on their children, humiliating children by shouting at them or degrading them in front of others, or embarrassing them by criticizing coaches and officials,' the report said. 'Most participants in the research believed junior players could describe an "ugly" parent incident, many of which would be about their own parents' behaviour.'

Admittedly, obnoxious parents will find an outlet for their insecurity in non-sporting settings too. Just think of the clucking and bitching that goes on in the wings of school plays, or on graduation days. However, there's something about Sports Day that actively encourages boorishness. At such events, Daddy feels he's not being a proper parent unless he's shouting blue murder at his little angel. And this raises a broader question: Do those sporting optimists who hail competitive game-playing as a 'force for good' never wonder why other pastimes, and social activities, are relatively peace-loving? Why do art fans never square up to gallery curators after a disappointing show and tell them they need 'f**king glasses'? Why do you never see head-butting at book fairs? Why don't actors feign injury to make their co-stars look bad? Why, for heaven's sake, are rock stars less likely to get involved in bar fights than professional footballers?

Sports optimists sweep away such criticism with the blithe remark: 'It's not sport that's the problem. It is professionalism.' Or: 'It's commercialism.' Or: 'It's the corruption of the Corinthian spirit.' All nonsense. If there's one thing that's certain:

• THERE WAS NO GOLDEN AGE OF SPORTING PURITY •

You might like to think that a sport such as rugby has descended from noble beginnings ('a game for ruffians played by gentlemen') to a somewhat cynical exercise in violence. Or, you might be lured into thinking that today's educationalists have strayed from the original vision of the Muscular Christians – by putting too much emphasis on the 'Muscular' and not enough on the 'Christian'. But was it really any different in Dr Arnold's day? From the outset, rugby, and similar team sports, were largely seen as an avenue by which public schools could increase their prestige. Results were all-important, and they seemed to justify a high level of aggression – as indicated by the warfare-like descriptions of early games involving an oval ball at Rugby School.

Indeed, one wonders what commitment the Muscular Christians really had to Christianity. Theirs was a puzzling version of Jesus' creed, as highlighted by – among others – John Henry Newman. The theologian accused Charles Kingsley of being 'anti-intellectual' in a public spat that foresaw Newman's departure from the Anglican Church for the Catholic one.

If the Victorian era was not the 'golden age' of sport, morally speaking, then when was? Certainly not the Edwardian period as described by George Orwell – a product of such fine English institutions as Eton and Wellington College. Orwell regarded sport, in the words of one author, as 'a training ground for elitist bullies who would go on to use their experiences within sport to promote violence and conflict in later life'. The philosophy of the era, as Orwell saw it, was perhaps best captured in his essay 'Such, Such Were the Joys'. Here Orwell speaks of his experiences at St Cyprian's, an exclusive preparatory school in Sussex, where the pattern of life was 'a continuous triumph of the strong over the weak':

> Virtue consisted in winning: it consisted in being bigger, stronger, handsomer, richer, more popular, more elegant, more unscrupulous than other people – in dominating them, bullying them, making them suffer pain, making them look foolish, getting the better of them in every way. Life was hierarchical and whatever happened was right. There

were the strong, who deserved to win and always did win, and there were the weak, who deserved to lose and always did lose, everlastingly.

The mood of the time, with its macho, imperialist flavour, is also captured in the Edwardian volume, *Association Football and the Men Who Made It*, in which judge William Pickford reflected:

> When you can eliminate the spirit of the Anglo-Saxon from the national elements and substitute the mildness and patience of the Hindoo for it, we may perhaps arrive at playing football in a purely scientific manner, with no more physical danger than is incurred in a game of lawn tennis or golf. When that day arrives may I have laid down my pen and rested my bones in their last pilgrimage, for I don't want to be present.

Now, turn the clock forward and consider the time just prior to what is commonly called the 'professional era' – to, let's say, 1976. Was this the golden age of sporting virtue? In rugby, many believe so. Gareth Edwards, J.P.R. Williams and Co. were mesmerising spectators – and they weren't getting a penny for it. But was the game any 'cleaner' than it is today? Stamping, punching, eye-gouging and other such offences – offences that would horrify today's audiences with the availability of close-up camera shots

– were commonplace in international matches. Former Irish rugby international John Robbie, who played in that 'golden age', says people have forgotten the 'savage' running battles that used to take place in Test matches. 'Rugby is cleaner than it has ever been by a factor of about a million,' he says, recalling a notorious match between the New Zealand regional side, Southland, and a touring Irish team of which he was part in 1976. The match attracted widespread comment in the media, including this leader article in a New Zealand newspaper:

> Too often … nasty encounters are occurring right at the beginning of matches, long before the game itself has had a chance to generate its own hostility. They come from hostility of quite a different sort – dressing-room hostility built up by coaches, captains and the players themselves as a kind of non-alcoholic Dutch courage for the fight ahead. Instead of the players going out to play against men they like and respect, for the good of the game, they are deliberately brainwashing themselves to dehumanise the opposition and treat them as rugby cannon fodder.

A close observer of sport would similarly comment in the late 1970s: 'One of the most disturbing features of modern sport, especially contact sport at top level, is the permission and even encouragement of behaviour verging on psychopathic.' (Recall, this was the era in which people were playing for 'pride' rather than anything as grubby as money.) It could be argued, then, that professionalism has created an altogether more humane sporting environment. For one thing, the incidence of serious injuries – like paralysing neck-breaks – has declined (albeit this may be partly thanks to improved medical care at sports fixtures).

Before criticising professionalism, consider too how the sporting greats of old really behaved. Cricket's 'pillar of the establishment' W.G. Grace was a notorious bender of the rules. He is perhaps most famous for once turning down an official's instructions to walk, when clean-bowled, with the words: 'They came to see me bat, not to see you umpire.' Today's footballers are commonly labelled prima donnas. But are they any less self-regarding than the likes of soccer legend Pelé, who has said of Robinho, one of the latest Brazilian superstars: 'He is the best. He reminds me of me'? Think too of J.P.R. Williams, the pin-up boy of Welsh rugby's amateur heyday. Apart from his prolific scoring record, he is probably most famous for his role in the 1974 Lions tour of South Africa, where he was seen chasing a player around the field in order to throttle him following the touring side's infamous '99' call to violence.

Yes, you can find the odd 'Corinthian' character from yore – Eric Liddell, for instance, the 'Flying Scotsman' and Christian missionary immortalised in *Chariots of Fire*.

But you can find similar characters today too. Take, for example, the otherworldly British triple-jumper Jonathan Edwards who, like Liddell, refused to compete on a Sunday because it clashed with his religious beliefs (admittedly Edwards eventually reneged on this stance). Individual acts of 'Corinthianism' are also not hard to find. Snooker legend Stephen Hendry sometimes refused 'free balls' that were awarded to him in tournament matches as a sporting gesture towards opponents. Former Liverpool striker Robbie Fowler once famously pleaded with a referee not to award him a penalty after he had been tackled in a scoring position.

It is a mistake, then, to associate amateurism with 'good' and professionalism with 'bad' – as though an athlete becomes impure as soon as he, or she, is paid for his deeds.

• AN AMATEUR IS JUST A PROFESSIONAL •
IN THE WRONG BUSINESS

For a start, amateurism in sport has always been a deceit. Just as Kingsley's rugby was never very Christian, de Coubertin's Olympic Games were never far removed from 'professional' ideals. The earliest Olympians drew on financial support from either their own personal income or else a wealthy benefactor in order to compete. And many an 'amateur' icon embraced performance-related pay. On his first tour of Australia in 1873–74, W.G. Grace reputedly extracted a fee of £1,500 from the organisers, the equivalent of well over £100,000 at present values.

D.J. Taylor – drawing on the poetry of Philip Larkin – traces the end of amateurism to the 1960s, claiming: 'Rather like sexual intercourse, it turns out, professionalism proper took root between the end of the *Chatterley* ban and the Beatles' first LP.' But it would be truer to say that, professionalism – like sex – has always been with us. It's just that we started giving it proper acknowledgement only 40-odd years ago. Aside from being paid – often indirectly or on the sly – the earliest athletes shared with their descendants an obsessive, competitive drive. Despite the various platitudes voiced by Muscular Christians, sport has always been organised with a focus on the winning over the taking part. This goes even for the Olympic Games in its earliest manifestations. As Peter McIntosh points out, in his groundbreaking *Fair Play: Ethics in Sport and Education* (1979): 'The Olympic Games … while preaching and promoting humanism, amateur ideals, equality of terms in competition, friendship in the contest and other human values are, at the same time, in living up to their motto *Citius, Altius, Fortius* [Swifter, Higher, Stronger], contributing to the professionalisation of sport.'

The truth is that athletes don't do bad things because they are paid. Rather, they do bad things because they are athletes. The culture of competitive game-playing encourages them to commit what would normally be considered moral transgressions.

Many researchers in the field tend to pussy-foot around this issue, typically blaming 'over-competitiveness', 'professionalism', or more creatively 'excessive professionalism' for the crimes of sport. They seem loath to blame sport *per se*, and some will engage in any amount of verbal gymnastics to deflect criticism away from sporting practices. One exception is Jay Coakley, a US-based sociologist who spent over 30 years studying the behaviour of elite sports performers at the University of Colorado, Colorado Springs. He argues that 'athletes are systematically encouraged to over-conform to a unique set of norms embodied in what might be called a "sport ethic".' He lists these norms as follows: '(a) Being an athlete involves making sacrifices for "the game"; (b) Being an athlete involves striving for distinction; (c) Being an athlete involves accepting risks and playing through pain; and (d) Being an athlete involves refusing to accept limits in the pursuit of possibilities.' Coakley writes:

> It is seldom recognized that many ethical problems and forms of deviance in sports are not due to athletes denying or rejecting social values or norms. Instead, they are due to athletes accepting and committing themselves without question or reservation to the normative guidelines that constitute what might be called the 'ethic' of many sports cultures today ...

His comments on performance-enhancing drugs are particularly noteworthy:

> The use of these substances is not the result of defective characters among athletes, or the existence of too many material rewards in sports, or television coverage, or exploitation by coaches and managers, or moral weakness among athletes ... After all, users are often the most dedicated and committed people in sports! Instead ... most substance use and abuse is clearly tied to an over-commitment to the sport ethic itself; it is grounded in over-conformity – the same type of over-conformity that leads injured distance runners to continue training even when training may cause serious physical problems, and American football players to risk their bodies through excessively violent physical contact week after painful week in the NFL, and figure skaters to risk leg injuries by doing triple after triple after quadruple jumps in their quests for 'perfection' ...

The logic of Coakley's thesis is that competitive sport is a somewhat dangerous and unhealthy pursuit, best approached with caution. Unfortunately, you won't find him, or, indeed, anyone else in an athletic-collegiate setting, stating this openly. Researchers in the field are too eager to give sport the benefit of the doubt. In blaming 'over-conformity' to the sports ethic rather than mere 'conformity', Coakley specifically creates yet another barrier to criticism that sport can hide behind. In practice, the two terms are indistinguishable (certainly, Coakley offers no means of distinguishing between them). After all, how can you play sport – and play it successfully – without 'excessively' making sacrifices, striving for distinction and/or refusing to accept limits?

All things considered, perhaps the kindest statement you can make about sport is the following:

• **THE MORE SERIOUSLY YOU TAKE SPORT THE MORE** •
LIKELY YOU ARE TO DO HARM TO YOURSELF OR OTHERS

How blasé should you be about winning? Just how far should you regard sport as 'only a game'? In answer, I often think of my mother – a saintly woman, and uncompetitive to a fault. In family games of Monopoly, she hates it when an opponent lands on one of her properties, all the more so if she happens to have placed a few houses, or, God forbid, a hotel, on it. (Her aversion to charging her children rent has always extended to the family home too.) An accomplished show-jumper in her youth, she has since become somewhat embarrassed by her one-time sporting prowess, as though it belonged to a criminally-vain former self. The last time I played tennis against her she called one of my balls 'in' when it was 'out' so I wouldn't be disappointed at losing an evenly-fought rally.

A lesser competitive instinct one might find only among highly-trained Buddhists, the following tale being told of the Dalai Lama as a boy. Walking through the Tibetan capital city of Lhasa with a visiting Nordic academic, the spiritual leader stopped before a friendly game of volleyball. The game perplexed the Swedish professor, as the players all wore the same coloured uniform, and batted the ball back and forth over the net apparently without keeping score. When asked about the scene, the Dalai Lama explained: 'Everyone tries to keep the ball in the air. That's all there is to it. When the ball hits the ground it's a sad moment for everyone, and you'll notice how they take a moment to console the person responsible.' The Western professor replied: 'In our country, we divide into opposing sides and then we try to make the others miss the ball.' As the story goes, the Dalai Lama found this quite distressing:

'But the ball must hit the ground all the time.'
'Your Highness, why are you weeping?' the professor rejoined.
'Such a way to play with the human spirit,' sobbed the boy. Deeply shaken, he went to his room to pray.

Admittedly, not all Buddhists share the Dalai Lama's anti-competitive spirit. For many a Buddhist, golfer Tiger Woods among them, serious sport is perfectly compatible with the principles of their faith. In the introduction to a special report on 'sport and society' in 2006, Soka Gakkai International – a Buddhist network of 15 million people, including former Italian footballer Roberto Baggio – commented: 'Besides its obvious beneficial effects on physical health, sport can act as a powerful inculcator of positive values and attitudes, as athletes themselves describe.'

On the whole, the world's other major religions are similarly upbeat about sport – in each case, however, with certain caveats. 'Sport, *when practised in the right way*, can be an educative tool and a means to foster human and spiritual values,' Pope Benedict XVI once remarked (italics are my own). The qualifying clause in his statement reflects the thinking of his predecessor, who famously played as a goalkeeper for his local soccer team when growing up in Poland. 'In addition to a sport that helps people, there is another that harms them,' said Pope John Paul II. 'In addition to a sport that enhances the body, there is another that degrades it and betrays it; in addition to a sport that pursues noble ideals, there is another that looks only for profit; in addition to a sport that unites, there is another that divides.'

Despite his reservations about competitive game-playing, the late pontiff saw fit to establish an office for 'Church and Sport' in 2004 to explore the latter's potential as 'an instrument of peace and brotherhood'. A somewhat puzzling development, it illustrates that the Church is as susceptible as other organisations to romanticising the value of athletic vocations. (Indeed, if sport deserves an office of its own within the Vatican, then why not alcohol, for example, or rock music? Think of all the peaceful, brotherly unions for which drunk concert-goers are responsible.)

The first director of the office for Church and Sport was Father Kevin Lixey, an American priest who said he longed to see a kind of sport emerge 'that protects the weak and excludes no one, that frees young people from the snares of apathy and indifference, and arouses a healthy sense of competition in them … [and] which contributes to the love of life, teaches sacrifice, respect and responsibility, leading to the full development of every human person.' (How's that for wishful thinking?)

In Judaism, there has traditionally been some antipathy towards sport. Allied to that is a perception that Jews are somehow 'unsporty' by nature – a perception underlined by the following exchange from the 1980 comedy film *Airplane!*:

> AIR HOSTESS: 'May I offer you something to read?'
> PASSENGER: 'Yes, do you have something light?'
> AIR HOSTESS: 'How about this leaflet: Famous Jewish Sport Legends?'

Many a Jew would laugh at the above, but not so Max Nordau. A key figure in the late 19th-century Zionist movement, Nordau is credited with forming the doctrine of *Muskeljudentum*, or Muscular Judaism, at a time when its Christian counterpart was in vogue. Criticising what he perceived as the 'effeminacy' and nervousness of Jews, he called for an investment in Jewish-run sports facilities that 'will straighten us in body and character'. He wrote: 'We want to restore to the flabby Jewish body its lost tone, to make it vigorous and strong, nimble and powerful.' Thus was born the Maccabi movement, which spread around the world, creating over 100 sports clubs in Europe by the beginning of the First World War. The movement reversed an age-old antipathy towards sport within Judaism that stretched back as far as the 4th century BC, when the gymnasium was seen as a Hellenistic temple for the worship of false idols. In the words of one Jewish historian, theatres and circuses were once linked together in the Jewish mind 'as the very antithesis of "synagogue and school"'.

Today, there are no great philosophical debates within Judaism about sport, it being seen as a relatively benign activity. Within Islam, the picture is slightly more complex. There is a spectrum of views on the subject, reflecting the diverse nature of the Muslim world. At one extreme are the likes of the Taliban, who banned the popular pastime of kite-flying in Afghanistan because it supposedly clashed with the Qur'an and Shari'a law. The Taliban also prohibited hand-clapping during sports events, seeking in its place the chanting of 'God is great'. In addition, they banned women's sports – though this had more to do with their attitude towards women than towards sport *per se*. At the other extreme, what could be called moderate, or mainstream Muslims have enthusiastically embraced sport, taking pride in the successes of people like Muhammad Ali, Hicham El Guerrouj and Imran Khan (and arguably to a lesser degree in the triumphs of the occasional breakthrough woman athlete).

In between these two poles there are different shades of opinion. According to one US textbook on Muslim morals, the Prophet Muhammad recommends that followers engage in certain pursuits 'related to the martial arts, training Muslims for the battlefields of *jihad* in the cause of Allah'. The text explains that, under Islamic law, games like wrestling, foot-racing and archery are permissible, while dice, backgammon and any such game 'played with money which has an element of gambling' are *haraam* (forbidden). Inevitably, this view is contradicted elsewhere, with a different textbook on Islamic morals claiming that gambling is permissible on 'a camel, horse or elephant race' (which is just as well for the horseracing-mad United Arab Emirates royal family, who would otherwise face Islamic-style excommunication). The same text argues against wrestling, boxing or any other sport 'which endanger[s] life'. It continues: 'In Islam, sports are encouraged insofar as they are a means to build strong, healthy bodies. Sport must be treated as a means and not as an end; when sport becomes an end in itself it is prohibited.'

The latter point is somewhat ambiguous, but perhaps no more so than secular thinking in the field.

Philosophers of a liberal bent tend to reject an ethic of 'winning at all costs' but only for one of 'winning at some costs' – and ultimately the distinction between the two is rather vague. An academic spokesman for utilitarianism, for example, sets up a dichotomy between 'winning' and 'playing to win', and argues that players will, on average, maximise their happiness by aiming for the latter rather than former. The logic is sound in this regard: If neither of two players cares as much about victory as simply doing his best, then competition between the pair can produce a 'win-win' situation. In practice, however, 'doing your best' is invariably tied up with limiting, or obstructing, your opponent's chances of victory. A player 'doing his best' in a tennis match, for instance, will try to exploit his opponent's weaknesses, and minimise the exploitation of his own, so much so that he will become indistinguishable from a player who is simply aiming to win.

Here, again, we can reach a qualified conclusion:

THERE IS ONLY ONE WAY OF GUARANTEEING THAT YOUR
• PARTICIPATION IN SPORT DOES NOT CAUSE HARM, AND •
THAT IS TO AVOID TAKING THE PURSUIT SERIOUSLY

I say that the above statement is qualified because it may be *impossible* to participate in sport without taking it seriously. If that is the case, we could be compelled, ethically-speaking, to avoid sport altogether.

Probably the closest thing to non-competitive sport today is the Special Olympics, best described as a programme of activities for people with intellectual disabilities. With their motto 'Let me win but if I cannot win, let me be brave in the attempt', the 'games' are hotly contested by qualifying athletes. Yet the overall focus of the event is less on victory than on advancing personal development and building the self-esteem of all participants. As a result, few people watch the Special Olympics. According to conventional wisdom, it's simply not sport.

Sporting organisations are all too aware of the dark side of their games but, for obvious reasons, they choose not to highlight it. When forced to explain themselves, they point to codes of conduct that set out the manner in which sport should ideally be played. Yet such codes have about as much impact on sporting participants as a UN resolution expressing 'grave concern' has on rogue states. They are, in short, unenforceable. And, perhaps because of this, no one makes an effort to enforce them.

You may not be surprised to hear that Australia has one of the most comprehensive collections of voluntary sporting codes in the world. The codes, which are backed by the Australian government, apply to coaches, players and spectators. They include advice such as: 'Positive comments are motivational ... Never ridicule or yell at your child.' The documents are all very worthy, of course. But are they worth the paper they are written on? Were spectators to 'respect the decisions of officials', as the codes demand, it would mean an end to referee-baiting. And what self-respecting Ozzie sports fanatic would agree to that?

Other codes are either hopelessly optimistic or highly contradictory. The Council of Europe, for example, has a much-publicised code of ethics that, in typical European fashion, looks like it was drafted by a clutch of disparate nations speaking very different languages. The document calls for the promotion of 'fair play', which is defined very specifically as something that 'incorporates issues concerned with the elimination of cheating, gamesmanship, doping, violence (both physical and verbal), the sexual harassment and abuse of children, young people and women, exploitation, unequal opportunities, excessive commercialisation and corruption'. Funnily enough, 'issues' involving the abuse of men don't seem to be relevant to fair play. But this is just one of many beguiling aspects of the document.

One practical step might be to limit the competitive nature of players, through – for example – a prohibition on prize-giving. This is already popular in some primary schools, and is seen specifically as a means of allowing children to have some sort of pre-competitive school life. On the other hand, many parents believe 'friendly' games are poor preparation for surviving in the cut-throat world that Little Johnny will eventually have to face. Significantly, when a primary school in the West Midlands wrote to parents in 2003 asking them not to attend the annual sports day because their presence might 'embarrass' athletically-ungifted students, there was a major parental backlash. 'This is political correctness gone mad,' one parent told the BBC. 'Children don't become scarred for life because they lose the egg and spoon race.'

Whatever the chances of limiting competition among youths, it's a complete non-runner among adults. Some time ago, college football authorities in the US forbade athletic training during certain seasons to allow players to concentrate on their academic studies. But colleges regularly breach the spirit, and the letter, of the law by getting their athletes to train off-campus, or in informal settings. Monitoring training levels might just be possible within the confines of a particularly strict boarding school. But beyond that – looking at the national or the international picture – there can be nothing other than a free-for-all. On a visit to China ahead of the 2008 Olympics, British Olympic rower, Matthew Pinsent, reported that Chinese gymnastics coaches were beating their young charges during practice sessions. But even if the allegations had been confirmed, there was no way of acting upon them.

Another proposal – and one that psychologists are particularly fond of – is to try to train athletes to resist the temptation to do harm to themselves and others. 'Coaches should first try to create a positive moral environment for their athletes by standing back from "victory at all costs", trying to be "moral mentors", and stimulating pro-social behaviour among athletes,' argues one team of French therapists. 'At the same time, young athletes should learn to develop self-regulatory skills in order to ward off social pressure, whether it comes from their coaches, their team-mates, their hypothetical financial partners, or from supporters.'

Worthy ideas, perhaps. But when would they ever be put into practice in the current results-obsessed sporting environment? As Professor Moran points out, there is scant debate at any level of sport over questions of morality. 'No one does that kind of work – exploring what athletes do during games. No one says, "When you had an opportunity to score a winning try, or a winning goal, you could have cheated and got away with it." There is nobody debating those sorts of points with athletes,' he says.

One can't help feeling that the lack of debate suits the sporting authorities. After all, the last thing they need is for athletes to be independently-minded. Were athletes to think critically about their relationship with sport, they might – for example – come to the conclusion that winning isn't everything. And where would gate receipts lie then?

With pressure mounting from sponsors to 'clean up' the image of sport, governing bodies are increasingly trying to deflect attention onto the supposed sins of individual athletes and – in tandem – away from problems inherent to competitive game-playing. Displaying devious inconsistency, and a judgemental streak of which the Spanish Inquisition would be proud, the authorities are today clamping down on practices that are either trivial (like footballers taking off their jerseys after scoring goals), or largely irrelevant (like sportspeople using recreational drugs).

The hypocrisy runs deep, and it's that to which we now turn.

CHAPTER 3

STRING 'EM UP: SPORT, CHEATING AND JUDGEMENTALISM

'I want to win an Olympic gold medal. After that I don't care.'
    sprinter Ben Johnson before the 100-metre final at the
                       1988 Olympic Games in Seoul

'Extreme justice is extreme injustice' (Summum jus, summa injuria)

                                             Cicero

The date, 27 September 1988, the day Ben Johnson was stripped of his 100-metre Olympic gold medal after testing positive for steroids, was truly a landmark occasion in sport. It was not, as some claim rather melodramatically, 'the day sport died' (sport has plainly lived on). Nor was it 'the end of an age of innocence'. (Johnson's positive test came after fifteen years of systematic and quite brazen doping by the East Germans. By the time of the Seoul Games, eleven months before the fall of the Berlin Wall, there should have been no innocents left.) No, Ben Johnson's case was exceptional for one reason, and one reason alone: it set a precedent. A prominent athlete – a veritable superstar who had just become the world's fastest man – was caught taking drugs and punished.

To prove this was no show trial, no case of victimisation, the Olympic movement and its affiliate bodies (which, together, represented the bulk of organised sport) had no choice from that moment on but to catch drug cheats and punish them. Or, at least, to create the appearance of doing so. 27 September 1988 is best described, then, as the dawn of a new era of crime and punishment. Or more accurately, perhaps, a new era of puritanism. To all intents and purposes, a crusade had begun to rid sport of all cheating.

Just where you stand on Ben Johnson may well reflect your broader philosophical or political viewpoint. 'Liberals', for want of a better word, will dwell on the fact that the Canadian sprinter was not the first – nor indeed the last – athlete to test positive for banned substances. They will cite the fact that four of Johnson's seven rivals in the 100-metre final – a race dubbed in some quarters as 'the most corrupt race ever' – subsequently failed drug tests. They, and perhaps there aren't many of them, may refer to Johnson's relative youth (he was 26 at the time of the race), and to the fact that he was manipulated to some degree by his handlers. (Even IOC Vice-President Dick Pound admitted at the time: 'Johnson probably wouldn't know what a steroid is.') 'Conservatives', on the other hand, will argue that you must make an example of rule-breakers. They'll say that Johnson deserves no sympathy because he changed his story so many times, from an initial position of denying the charges to a later, robust defence of drug-taking. ('Regardless of what I did, I am still the best sprinter of all time,' the Canadian said a few years ago. 'Most people loved the entertainment and know the game.') Conservatives, moreover, may refer to Johnson's relative maturity (he was 31 by the time he tested positive for drugs on a second occasion, leading to a lifetime ban from the sport). They might also make the case that, while temptation was put in Johnson's way, he could at any stage have said 'No'.

I can see both sides of the argument but I've always been more sympathetic to the liberals: (1) Because I myself have cheated in sport on occasion, and have got away with it (an erroneous call in a tennis tournament once comes to mind); and (2) Because I used to be a big fan of 1988 Olympic triple-gold medallist Florence Griffith-Joyner despite having serious doubts about how she managed to develop her incredible muscular physique. Under the circumstances, it would be a bit hypocritical of me to condemn Ben Johnson.

I do believe I'm not alone in having some sympathy for the Canadian sprinter. Simon Barnes, chief sportswriter at *The Times*, recently named Johnson's 'win' as the second-greatest sporting moment of all time (after Steve Redgrave's fifth successive Olympic gold medal in 2000). 'That run, the electrifying run, it still affects me, with its awful perfection,' Barnes writes in his book, *The Meaning of Sport*. 'The most perfect single piece of sport I have ever seen.' Whatever you may think about giving Johnson's 'achievements' their appropriate recognition, there was something unappealing – unbalanced even – about the overall reaction to his cheating. The Olympic movement portrayed him as a bogeyman, as a symbol of professionalism gone wrong. Describing the incident as a 'national embarrassment', Canada's sports minister Jean Charest said Johnson should be banned from ever representing the national team again. Mention of his West Indies heritage became more frequent in the media. A cartoon in one Canadian newspaper summed up the mood at the time, using the following series of mock-headlines: 'CANADIAN SPRINTER WINS GOLD IN 100 METRES!' 'JAMAICAN-CANADIAN ATHLETE TESTS POSITIVE FOR STEROIDS!' 'JAMAICAN ATHLETE STRIPPED OF GOLD MEDAL.'

Even the manner in which Johnson was informed of the result had an unsavoury flavour. The athlete was bundled out of the Olympic village and checked in under a pseudonym to a hotel bedroom, where the IOC suddenly told him to hand his gold medal back. Carol Anne Letheren, *chef de mission* of the Canadian delegation, recalled: 'He [Johnson] was in a state of shock ... He still did not comprehend the situation.' In the hours, weeks and months that followed, the entire sporting establishment – the media, administrators, politicians, and even fellow athletes – tried to put as much distance as possible between the disgraced athlete and themselves. Yet all of them had some role to play in creating the thing that was Ben Johnson, just as I had some role to play in creating

'Flo-Jo'. She was literally a pin-up girl on my bedroom wall, and hers was the Olympic 100-metres final that I – as a teenage schoolboy – had longed to see most. (I can still recall bedding down in front of the TV with an alarm clock set for the 4am final broadcast live from South Korea.)

I didn't know if she was on drugs, and deep down, I suspect, I didn't care. It mattered to her, though. Griffith-Joyner died of a suspicious heart attack at the age of 38.

Buddhists claim we must share responsibility for each other's sins. I'm not sure I fully agree. But I do believe we need to acknowledge our own role, however small, in facilitating or encouraging wrong-doing. For the world of sport to isolate Johnson and say 'He is nothing to do with us', would be like the town of Springfield turning on Bart Simpson and saying 'We don't know how he turned out this way'. If ever there was a product of his environment, it was Johnson.

Which brings us back to 27 September 1988. Had the IOC any other option but to disqualify the Canadian and send him home in disgrace? Certainly not, if it wished to maintain the illusion of fairness in sporting contests. That illusion is of critical importance to sponsors, and indeed to the vast majority of fans. It's what makes sport 'authentic' in the minds of countless spectators.

An illusion, however, is an illusion. Sport is not entirely fair, and it never will be. Indeed, sport without the presence of cheating is not sport at all.

• CHEATING IS A KEY PART OF SPORT •

This comment is not meant as a criticism of sport. It's simply a fact that self-interested 'bending the rules' will always arise in competition, as the flip-side of 'sportsmanship'. Whether it's using prohibited substances, 'diving' in football, or declining to call 'out' a ball that had gone unseen by a tennis referee so you can replay the rally and save a match point (I'm still racked with guilt!), cheating is impossible to eradicate entirely. Unless, that is, you create a sterile and carefully managed, sporting environment. And were that possible, would it be desirable? A world without vice is a world without freedom of choice. And it's also a world without virtue.

It's clear that sportsmanship, in the sense of behaving altruistically – or charitably – in a competitive context, is nothing unless it means subverting the law. When Chris Evert overruled an umpire who had given a point in her favour during a 1977 Wimbledon Championship match, she was refusing to yield to authority in no less a way than John McEnroe used to during his famous on-court eruptions. The fact that Evert went on to lose the game in question, and the match, made her action all the more rebellious. Take, as a more clear-cut example of sportsmanship, a tennis player who sees her opponent's ball go out. She *knows* she has won the point, but her opponent thought the ball might have been in, and is disappointed by the 'out' call. The player who won the rally decides to replay the point. Her behaviour is rightly called 'sporting', in a virtuous sense. But at the same time it amounts to obstructing the ends of justice. The outcome she favoured was not the fair one. It was not the outcome which she had a duty to uphold under the rules of tennis.

Another example of sportsmanship comes from a Premiership game in December 2000 between West Ham and Everton. It was 1–1 at Goodison Park and the Hammers were chasing a vital away win against a team of fellow relegation strugglers. As the ball was chipped into the Everton box, the Toffees' goalkeeper Paul Gerrard turned awkwardly and, seemingly injured, fell to the ground. At that moment, West Ham striker Paolo Di Canio lined up to receive the ball. But instead of heading it towards the net for an almost certain score, he caught the ball and ran straight to the fallen player to see if he was alright. Fifa awarded Di Canio a 'Fair Play' award the following year, describing the gesture as 'a special act of good sportsmanship'. But was it in his gift to do what he did? Many West Ham fans didn't think so, arguing after the game that he had no right to catch the ball. Indeed, technically, he should have received a booking from the referee. The West Ham manager Harry Redknapp described the gesture as 'amazing' in a not-altogether complimentary sense. 'I've not had a go about it,' Redknapp said ever-so charitably. 'What you will never know is if Everton would have done the same thing.' Others were less restrained in their response. 'When Paolo did his act of sportsmanship he must have forgot about all the other people he would or could have hurt … More people are now hurt by the demotion, and possibly out of work … Do the job you are paid for first, then think about the plaudits,' railed one correspondent on a BBC website.

Whatever the rights and wrongs of Di Canio's actions, one thing is clear: He disobeyed the rules. Is it just a coincidence that Di Canio has a record of transgressions, including the pushing over of a referee in a Premiership game in 1998? What may apply for one player certainly applies for the whole of sport: You can't have the good without the bad.

It could be argued that the introduction of more rules and regulations in sport may actually be reducing the incidence of 'sportsmanship'. Athletes are perhaps less free to be sporting in an ethical sense today – just as they are less free to be unsporting. Certainly, one can see a reduction in the number of 'characters' in professional sport. Rebels like McEnroe, Jimmy Connors, George Best and Eric Cantona seem to belong to a remote and less constrained past. Thanks to the ever-increasing scrutiny of outsiders, professional footballers behave less like the liberated pop stars they surely dreamt of becoming, than city stockbrokers, complete with mock-Tudor mansions and flashy motors. Soon, it appears, all sports will be as rule-obsessed as golf, in which raising your baseball cap on the eighteenth green counts as a radical gesture.

There is a strong case for saying that sport isn't meant to be governed by hard-and-fast rules. Laws are for real life, whereas sport is primarily a field for legal experimentation, rule-bending and moral ambiguity; so the argument runs. This thinking used to be popular in ancient times, as illustrated by ulama, an Aztec ball game dating from 2000 BC, which operated by a set of playing directions that were not fully understood by its participants. Ambiguity was built into the game, which incorporated *veedors*, or elders, acting as arbiters in the case of a disputed call.

Such games were less about the result than the manner of play. Closer to art than pure competition, they allowed people to win with shame and lose with honour. And this is something, incidentally, which tallies with the sort of sport I played as a child. On the road where I grew up, there was a common practice of allowing a cheat to win for the price of a tainted reputation. If someone insisted at unreasonable length that they were 'in' when in fact they were 'out' in a game of rounders, for example, he or she would be allowed to play on, on the basis that other participants were 'letting the baby cheat off'.

It's largely a matter of taste as to whether you like your sport to be an exact competition or an experimental spectacle; whether you like golf or ulama, for example. To the likes of Sepp Blatter, ulama is the game from hell. It's about as marketable as potholing – and, perhaps as a result, is today played in only a handful of locations in Mexico. Blatter and his ilk wouldn't like ulama for another reason: It gives a third party absolute control over the outcome of games. While modern-day *veedors* are proclaimed to be independent, they are increasingly having to answer to power-hungry governing bodies. Twenty years ago, the English cricket umpire Merv Kitchen was asked about a controversial ruling he had made in a game. 'What goes on in the middle is our business,' he replied. '[It's] nothing to do with anyone else.' Today, Kitchen's view is highly antiquated. Referees in all codes must be 'accountable' (read 'subservient') to their employers. This was particularly evident in the case of Australian cricket umpire Darrell Hair, who controversially accused a Pakistani team of ball-tampering in a Test match in 2006 – a ruling that caused the game to be abandoned after the Pakistanis walked off the field in a huff. Hair was subsequently raked over the coals, and banned from umpiring international matches. His crime was a very modern one. It's a crime that is almost impossible for a referee to defend: inadvertently bringing embarrassment onto the game.

In the push for certainty in sport, decision-making is not only becoming more centralised, it's becoming more conservative. The first instinct of any governing body is to ban, rather than to permit. This can be seen especially in sport's approach to disabled athletes. Such athletes are constantly, and usually for mean-minded reasons, refused special permission from sporting authorities to use certain technologies or equipment that would allow them to compete against their able-bodied peers. Despite having a serious leg impediment, golfer Casey Martin was refused permission by the Professional Golfers' Association to use a golf cart in championship tournaments. (Martin had to go to the courts to get the decision overturned.) The US Youth Bowling Council once excluded a girl with cerebral palsy from playing in its competitions because she used a ramp to help direct her shots. The world athletics organisation, the IAAF, has tried to stop double-amputee sprinter, Oscar Pistorius, from competing in able-bodied games including the Beijing Olympics. So what if the runner's leg-blades compensated to some degree for his lost limbs? What right-thinking sports fan did not want to see him run? To a certain type of sporting purist, there should be no exception to the rules. But instead of being such a stickler, why not embrace the spirit of those informal games that I, for one, used to play in my youth? Such games, in the words of a like-minded nostalgic, 'are played with whoever shows up ... The rules are freely revised to take into account the number of players, the playing field ..., the level of skill, and anything else considered important.'

A more pertinent question is whether introducing more rules leads to less cheating – because if a correlation cannot be established, then why have rules in the first place? While it's dangerous to make sweeping assumptions, what appears to have happened over time is that cheating has not declined in sport. Rather, it has evolved. Some years ago, Fifa introduced a ban on tackling from behind – a pitch intervention that was mainly used by players as a defensive mechanism. The form of tackle was quickly phased out. But, around the same time, a new, more subtle form of behaviour suddenly exploded in football – namely shirt-pulling – which basically served the same purpose as 'tackling from behind' in that it stopped an opponent in his or her tracks.

There's no hard evidence to show that athletes are cheating any less today than in bygone times. However, it does look like they are using more evolved forms of cheating – and arguably that *is* progress. Instead of trying to put an opponent off his game by threatening to break his legs, a common enough tactic among professional footballers twenty years ago, a player today might take a leaf out of Marco Materazzi's book and wind up a rival through some tactless reference to one of his female relatives (as the Italian did so successfully against Zinedine Zidane in the 2006 World Cup Final.)

The proliferation of drugs in sport may be seen as one aspect of this evolution. The likes of human growth hormones (HGH) could be described as very much 'new school cheating', compared to the 'old school' of, say, Tonya Harding who admitted to scheming about injuring one of her opponents at the 1994 US figure-skating championships. Compared to Harding-esque breaches of the rules, drugs at least have the advantage of risking physical harm only to the cheater, as opposed to the cheatee. Funnily enough, though, the world of sport isn't keen to describe doping as in any way 'progressive' – and we will ask why in a moment. But, first, return to the question of whether rules generally do the job they are meant to.

● ATHLETES ARE NOT GETTING DIRTIER, ●
FANS ARE GETTING MORE JUDGEMENTAL

Perhaps the most we can say is that new rules in sport have helped to reduce the incidence of certain, dangerous forms of cheating – like physically injuring opponents in an illegal fashion. As discussed in the last chapter, there is evidence to suggest that excessive violence is lower in professional ranks, where regulation is higher, than in amateur ones. Despite that, or perhaps because of it, people today are increasingly critical of professional athletes. Relatively minor transgressions are treated as capital offences by a growing lobby of pitch-side pundits. The trend is, in fact, replicated in broader society where falling rates of serious crime have led to growing intolerance for petty offences such as vandalism. In Britain, anti-social behviour orders were introduced at the very time that crime rates were at a record low. Louise Casey, director of the Blair government's anti-social behaviour unit, told *The Economist* magazine in 2005: 'As crime has fallen, it has opened up some spare capacity to worry about litter, graffiti and abandoned cars.'

In sport, intolerance for petty offences has similarly risen with declining rates of what might be called capital crimes. Consider, for example, how the British media got itself worked into a frenzy at the 2006 Fifa World Cup over nothing as serious as a violent tackle but, rather, a wink. When Wayne Rooney got sent off in England's game against Portugal, one of his opponents, Cristiano Ronaldo, winked at the Portuguese subs' bench – an act perceived as either a celebration of Rooney's red card, or an indication that a devious plot to 'wind up' Rooney had proved successful. Whether either perception was accurate, it was *only a wink*. It surely didn't deserve a prolonged hate campaign in the British tabloids, which included the *Sun* producing a dart board out of the face of what the newspaper called 'the Portuguese nancy boy'.

What, moreover, did Ronaldo ever do to deserve the sort of abuse levelled at him by Eamon Dunphy, Ireland's most prominent sports pundit and the ghost-writer of Roy Keane's biography? Dunphy has described Ronaldo's admittedly somewhat annoying dribbling style as 'the most wicked thing in the game'. 'Ronaldo is a puffball who has never done it on the big occasion ... Ronaldo's a waste of space.' These are among Dunphy's more mild pronouncements on the Portuguese winger, who developed a reputation for 'going down easily' during the 2006 World Cup. Many others clearly share Dunphy's view. The phrase 'I hate Cristiano Ronaldo' produces more Google hits than 'I hate Osama bin Laden'. There have been at least two internet websites set up as receptacles for personalised abuse against the Portuguese player.

An interesting feature of such criticism is that it fails to take into account Ronaldo's relative youth. He was only

21 years old at the time of the World Cup, a highly emo-tive occasion which must have tested anyone's composure to the limit. Perhaps he can be criticised for diving but – like other forms of anti-social behaviour – it's something that players tend to grow out of. Surely, he shouldn't be condemned as a human being for a few youthful indiscre-tions, especially when he has displayed rare maturity in other areas – for instance by doing valuable charity work in East Timor?

Mean-spirited judgementalism seems to be the stock response today not just to outright cheating but to mis-takes. In the same tournament as Ronaldo's wink, English referee Graham Poll made a well-publicised error, for-getting to send off a player after showing him two yel-low cards. A match reporter on the Guardian Unlimited website described the referee as 'a complete clown', and much, much worse. Within hours of the final whistle in the Australia–Croatia game, an internet blog site had been set up entitled 'Graham Poll – get the f**k out of Germany'. It was a portent of things to come as the referee was ridiculed in the international press. The *Sun*'s head-line, 'POLL'S THREE CARD THICK', was relatively charitable under the circumstances. As the criticism mounted, Fifa president Sepp Blatter stuck the boot in. 'I have to say I'm not surprised about the reaction,' he said. 'We have had four officials [the referee and his three assistants] and what is not understandable is that nobody intervened. It's like a black-out ... There are people there and one of them should have intervened and run on to the field and said, "Stop, stop". Fifa subsequently dropped Poll from its refereeing panel (or sent him home early, depending on what spin you like to put on it). When Poll returned to the UK he found himself being ridiculed by fans who were neither Croatian nor Australian. 'World Cup and you've f**ked it up' was the chant that rang out at football stadiums up and down England whenever he was officiating. He said such abuse was a key factor in his decision to retire from the game prematurely in June 2007.

The sort of puritanism that helped to hound Poll from his job appears only to be getting worse. Reporting on the 2007 Champions League Final between Liverpool and AC Milan, *Sunday Telegraph* football correspondent Patrick Barclay accused the referee Herbert Fandel of making an 'inexcusable' mistake, specifically by blowing the final whistle with '16 seconds' of added time to run. While Fandel didn't admit to an error, Barclay railed: 'There was no matter of opinion involved. It was a matter of fact, as serious as (if not more than) Graham Poll's showing of three yellow cards to Josip Simunic of Croatia in the World Cup ... Fandel's negligence cheated the competition, the spectators and the viewing audience as well as Liverpool. He should not be awarded another big occasion for a while.' So now, according to the high priests of Fleet Street, a relatively minor time-keeping mistake warrants demotion. It's just as well the same exacting standards of punctuality aren't demanded elsewhere or, let's face it, there wouldn't be a journalist left in a job.

In the world of heightened judgementalism that now envelops sport, 'doing your best' is no defence. In a European Championships qualifier in October 2006, the then relatively new England manager Steve McClaren experimented with a 3-5-2 team formation. McClaren obviously didn't set out to lose the game, but he did: 2–0 away from home. In hindsight, the experiment wasn't the best idea. England drew their next competitive fixture – another tough, away game. Already, however, McClaren had become a figure of ridicule. Four-letter words prefixed by the moniker 'ginger' became the order of the day. At the following game against Andorra in Barcelona, what newspapers described as the 'vast majority' of England's travelling support sang chorus after chorus of 'You'll be sacked in the morning' and 'Steve McClaren is a wanker'. 'Never, not Don Revie, Bobby Robson, or even Graham Taylor, has any England manager suffered such vicious, sustained and damning abuse,' *The Scotsman* remarked. 'It was extraordinary that a man as mild as McClaren could elicit such strong feelings in supporters,' commented Sam Wallace in the *Independent on Sunday*. 'Football supporters protesting en masse are a force that can still effect change in the game but Wednesday night was gripped with the mood of the lynch mob. They were fed up with football, but they were enjoying the thrill of the hunt.'

Contrast McClaren's experience to that, for example, of Walter Winterbottom, who managed the English side that was famously thrashed 6–3 by Hungary at Wembley in 1953. Both the media and the fans showed grace in defeat, hailing the victors with a cry of 'Well done chaps!', as David Winner describes it in *Those Feet: An Intimate History of English Football*. 'No British newspapers called the players, manager or selectors a "national disgrace", no one told Winterbottom "In the Name of God, Go", or printed pictures of him as a vegetable, hardly anyone even mentioned his tactical errors,' Winner notes.

The scenes at Barcelona (England, incidentally, *won* the game 3–0) were perhaps symptomatic of a wider contemporary disease. In today's world of tabloid-driven, manufactured outrage, celebrities and public figures from the late Princess Diana to Sven-Goran Eriksson are 'fair game' for abuse because of their wealth, or fame. Tony Blair rightly criticised this 'pack' mentality in one of his final speeches before leaving office. He said the media on occasion is 'like a feral beast, just tearing people and reputations to bits, but no one dares miss out.' What Blair neglected to mention was that in sport the abuse can be far more vicious and personalised than in politics. A Cabinet minister implicated in a dodgy arms deal is almost certain to recover his reputation quicker than an England footballer who gets himself sent off in a World Cup. Contemporary moralists bleat that the David Beckhams of this world deserve added abuse because of their privileged position. But this smacks of nothing more than petty jealousy. When someone says 'I don't like Beckham because he is a pampered millionaire', what he probably means is, 'I don't like Beckham because I wish I had his money.'

The irony is that despite being more catty than the ensemble of *Desperate Housewives*, the press corps feels unjustly ostracised by the very people whom they bitch about. Sports hacks today commonly grumble that their subjects are aloof and circumspect, if not downright hostile, to outsiders such as them. What's more, journalists frequently cite such aloofness as proof of the modern professional's supposed contempt for the ordinary man. But do you blame athletes for not pallying up to a group of individuals who are almost programmed to back-stab when things turn sour?

EXPECTING ATHLETES TO BE ROLE MODELS IS NONSENSICAL

It wouldn't be so bad if fans, and other such observers, limited their sanctimonious pontificating to on-field matters. But off-field affairs are also seen as rich territory for sermonising. The American basketball star Charles Barkley was once vilified for spitting on a nine-year-old girl who was watching him play a game (he said he was aiming at a different courtside fan who had allegedly racially abused him). Barkley knew he had done something wrong. He apologised, and later befriended the young girl and her family. But that didn't stop people from condemning him. Why? Because society decrees that professional athletes are meant to be paragons of virtue, or 'role models'. In a perverse reordering of moral responsibility, parents look to footballers, basketball stars and other such public figures to set a good example for their children.

'I'm not a role model,' Barkley famously said. 'Just because I dunk a basketball doesn't mean I should raise your kids.'

And that should be the last word on the subject.

Ironically, sports stars get it from both directions over their off-pitch behaviour. Some people criticise them for being too individualistic, and others blame them for being too conformist. A celebrity like Tiger Woods, for example, is widely praised for his charity work. But another section of the sporting gallery takes him to task for not being more outspoken about things like racism in golf. Woods is often compared unfavourably, in this regard, to Muhammad Ali – the last, great sporting outsider of a global stature. It's argued that while Ali wore his politics on his sleeve, Woods keeps his tucked away in his freshly-ironed slacks.

But why should we expect sports stars to commentate on politics any more than the rest of us? And, were they to start doing so, who would be the first in the queue to tell them to shut up? It's one thing Gary Neville speaking on, say, the need for more cancer research. But what about Paolo Di Canio speaking on 'the Jewish question'?

Or Catalan nationalist and Barça defender Oleguer Presas advocating secession from Spain? Or what about some homophobic athlete praising the practice of stoning gays to death? *Financial Times* journalist Michael Steinberger tapped into a popular sentiment in this field when he wrote: 'One of the more nauseating aspects of the modern cult of celebrity is the soap box it provides to the famous and the vacuous. If David Beckham and Posh Spice wade into the debate over Britain and the euro, forgive me if I fall down with laughter.' The experience of former England manager Glen Hoddle – sacked in 1999 after discussing his attitude towards religion and disabilities in a controversial newspaper interview – offers something of a warning to any sports personality who dares express his true opinions.

THE HALLMARK OF A FAN IS SOMEONE WHO EASILY TAKES OFFENCE

That sport should be associated with heightened judgementalism is hardly surprising. Sport is a theatre of exaggerated emotions, and these can be expressed in a positive or negative sense: in hero-worshipping athletes, or alternatively – as we have seen – demonising them. The stereotypical sports fan is not known for his even temper or sense of perspective. He feels compelled to eulogise when moderate praise is due, and to condemn when mild censure is in order. Either way, the definitive fan is unbalanced, as eager to give offence as to take it.

Ronaldo's wink is a case in point.

Another such case is Gary Neville's celebration at beating Liverpool at Old Trafford in January 2006. After one of his team-mates scored a 90th-minute winner in the game, Neville ran to face the visiting fans who had taunted him during the game, and went, in his own words, 'bananas'. Now, any normal person would just shrug off such gloating, but football fans are a different breed. The *Independent* reported: 'Toilets were smashed in the visitors' section of the ground and cars vandalised in the car parks outside' in scenes 'that had some witnesses recalling the hooligan-ravaged days of the early 1980s.' The police said Neville's celebration fuelled the violence, and they were probably right – for the stereotypical sports fan is easily riled. Paranoia is his mental default mode. He believes everyone is out to get him – or, by extension, his team: the media, the politicians, the officials, and, of course, fellow fans. Imagined slights are everywhere. A word out of turn is grounds for a conspiracy theory.

The kind of paranoia I am talking about can be seen in those members of the Tartan Army who believe the BBC has an anti-Scottish bias in its sports coverage. Or, indeed, in the likes of Austin Deasy, a former Irish government minister and patriotic horseracing fan, who once accused the BBC and Channel 4 of deliberately mispronouncing the names of Irish nags. So enraged was the sports buff that he raised the issue in Ireland's parliament, criticising a British commentator who dared to call 'Buachallan

Buidhe' (pronounced in Gaelic along the lines of 'book-aw-lawn bwidge-uh') as 'Buckalawn Buddy'. Describing such errors as 'racist', 'revolting', 'extraordinarily deroga-tory' and 'deliberately degrading', he called for an inter-governmental summit to be held on the issue, and for the guilty commentators to be punished. 'They make no attempt to get the name right. It is a deliberate slur on the Irish,' he ranted.

There's more than just raw patriotism behind this sort of outburst. There's a lack of perspective that belongs uniquely to sport. Genuine sports fans are inherently incapable of seeing the bigger picture. In South Africa, for example, there are attempts under way to increase the representation of 'players of colour' on the national rugby team. One of the chief advocates of such reform is Butana Komphela, the chairman of South Africa's parliamentary portfolio committee on sport, who argues – not without good reason – that the country would benefit more from a losing, multi-racial rugby team than a winning, almost entirely white one. 'We should be saying we are not going to win for the next five years while we transform so that one day when we do win, we all win as a country, with no black and white issues,' said Komphela in a newspa-per article penned shortly before the 2007 rugby World Cup. He was replying to the following question from a correspondent to the paper, presumably a Springbok supporter: 'What is it that you do not understand about winning?'

Whatever your views on the race issue in South Africa, the exchange tells you all you need to know about fans and their perspective on the world. To the average fan, nothing – absolutely nothing – matters more than victory.

Tellingly, fans can be much more narrow-minded than participants in sport. Where some conflict occurs, the fan tends to be the last to forgive. Rooney made peace with Ronaldo shortly after Winkgate, but those baying for the Portuguese player's blood chose to ignore this fact. Beckham suffered no recriminations from his team-mates for getting himself sent off in the 1998 World Cup. But there was no such magnanimity on the streets of London, where an effigy of the England midfielder was burnt outside a pub. Beckham subsequently received death threats in a hate campaign that took a full two years to die down.

In the Republic of Ireland, a football supporters' civil war erupted over Roy Keane's early return from the 2002 World Cup after clashing with national team manager Mick McCarthy. Fans today remain bitterly divided over the affair, with some staying doggedly loyal to Keane and others defending the stance of McCarthy and his chief lieutenant in the 'Saipan' bust-up, Niall Quinn. What many such bickering fans seem to overlook, however, is that all three of these particular individuals have since kissed and made up, and have even worked with one another without recrimination.

'In life, you have to move on,' said Keane in November 2006 when he became manager of Sunderland, a club chaired by his one-time arch-enemy Quinn. 'Life is too short.'

That's where Keane – and, indeed, Quinn and McCarthy – differ from the average fan, for whom 'moving on' is an anathema. The whole point of being a fanatic is that you don't waver in your opinion; you don't look at situations from both sides. For the definitive fan, perceived grievances fester for years, becoming part of the very lifeblood of your sporting faith.

One reason why participants in sport may be more forgiving than spectators is their relatively superior knowledge about the causes of a particular offence. When a cyclist is caught taking drugs, there tends to be no audible criticism from the peloton. Some regard this as a cowardly closing of ranks. But it's also possible that colleagues of the offending athlete, including drug-free colleagues, are reluctant to condemn because they are acutely aware of how easy it is to 'slip' at some stage of their career.

The pattern can be seen more clearly in contact sports such as rugby, where players tend to play down indiscretions on the basis that the boot may literally be on the other foot some other day. When, for example, Kiwi player Troy Flavell was caught on camera viciously eye-gouging Steve Sinkinson in a New Zealand club game in 1997, the first person to leap to his defence was the injured party. Sinkinson said he hadn't been aware of much foul play during the game – and on the basis of his appeals, Flavell's sentence was reduced from a one-year ban to just three weeks.

Players also appear to be more forgiving of refereeing errors than spectators are. That is, if former England goalkeeper David James is any guide. Reacting to the ever-increasing criticism of referees in the Premier League, James wrote: 'Let's not get distracted by the technology issue, or get all evangelical about squeezing every last human error out of refereeing … The thought of having the fuzzy edges taken away from football upsets me.'

But if fans are quicker to judge (and slower to forgive) than athletes, what about sports administrators? It's hard to generalise – for the only consistent feature in their thinking is inconsistency. Sometimes governing bodies turn a blind eye to cheating. Other times they scapegoat individuals for the crimes of an entire sport. The situation is complicated by the fact that there is a myriad of different sporting authorities, each one controlling its own fiefdom. UK Athletics, for example, is the national governing body for track and field in Britain. It's part-funded by UK Sport, which manages National Lottery money, and it's also affiliated to the IAAF, the international governing agency for the sport. The IAAF works closely with the IOC but they are independent organisations – as is the World Anti-Doping Authority (Wada). Thus, an athlete who tests positive for a banned substance might find themselves being cleared of wrong-doing by UK Athletics but subjected to a penalty by the IAAF, which in turn is adjudged to be too lenient by Wada.

The end result is a justice system best represented by a whirling roulette wheel rather than a finely balanced scale. It's the luck of the draw as to whether or not the governing body in your particular country, and in your particular sport, takes whatever crime you have committed seriously. In the same week in December 2006, for example, South African football bosses slapped a six-month ban on a leading player who tested positive for marijuana, while Pakistani cricket bosses chose not to punish two senior players who tested positive for steroids. Where's the logic in that?

Such apparent inconsistencies undermine the credibility of policing efforts in sport. Justice administered in an uneven or arbitrary fashion is perhaps worse than no justice at all. Why, to take but one example, did Manchester United's Eric Cantona get an eight-month ban from football for delivering a kung-fu kick on a match spectator, while his former team-mate Mark Bosnich got nine months for testing positive for cocaine? Surely harming another person is worse than harming yourself? Surely too, in a sporting context, use of performance-enhancing drugs is worse than use of recreational ones? Yet Maradona received identical bans (of fifteen months) for testing positive for cocaine, in 1991, and for ephedrine, in 1994.

It goes without saying that sporting authorities should take a stance against wrong-doing. But their actions must be even-handed. For one thing, they themselves should not shirk responsibility for their role in leading individual athletes astray. Nor should they shirk responsibility for rogue behaviour, including corruption and nepotism, in their own ranks. How exactly are 'white collar' offenders treated in sport? A football player found guilty of match-fixing is guaranteed a life ban. Yet clubs that bribe refs are always given a second chance. Particularly cynical double-standards were on full view during the 2006 Italian match-fixing scandal. The eighteen football officials who were chiefly implicated in the affair got bans from the sport ranging from three months to five years. And the four clubs at the centre of the scandal received what amounted to token penalties. Juventus was relegated from Serie A, but after grumbling about potential lost revenue it had an additional point deduction rescinded, thus enabling it to return to the top league after just one season. AC Milan was initially booted out of the Champions' League but on appeal this punishment was also rescinded, and the club went on to win the competition in May 2007, sending out, well, what sort of lesson to the world about ethics in sport?

Contrast these punishments to, for example, the indefinite ban on former champion jockey Kieren Fallon from racing in Britain due to allegations of involvement in race-fixing. (The ban was lifted after seventeen months when an Old Bailey judge ruled there was no case against him.) Contrast also the hearing AC Milan and Juventus got with that received by the likes of footballer Rio Ferdinand, who was hit with an eight-month ban in 2003 for missing a routine drugs test. The player's appeal for a lighter sentence was summarily dismissed, thus preventing him from a possible once-in-a-lifetime appearance in the European Championships. And yet, if anything, individual athletes should face lighter sentences than organisations for breaking similar rules, given the multiplier effect that bans have on generally short sporting careers. A season's relegation is a blip on the balance sheet for a top football club. But a season's ban from soccer is potentially career-ending for a player.

The only discernible pattern in sports justice is that offences in any way related to drugs are treated far more seriously than other crimes, acts of violence included. For the eye-gouging incident, Flavell was banned for three weeks. For testing positive to high levels of Salbutamol after a match in 2003, Irish rugby international Frankie Sheahan was banned for three months. (The initial ban was two years but it was reduced on appeal when Sheahan – an asthmatic – argued that the high reading was related to his use of a Ventolin inhaler and allied dehydration.)

Or, to give another example: Roy Keane earned a three-match ban and a fine of £5,000 for a knee-high challenge on Alf Inge Haaland in 2001. For admitting in his autobiography that he had deliberately sought to injure the

Norwegian, Keane got a further five-match ban and a fine of £150,000. In total, that meant a ban from football of roughly two months and a fine the equivalent of two to three weeks' wages for a quite calculated attack on an opponent. Now think of Ferdinand, who missed a drugs test because, he said, he was preoccupied with a house move. For the offence, he was slapped with a £50,000 fine and a full season's ban from football.

I'm not alone in feeling there's something a little skewed in such rulings. Reflecting in 2005 on the contrasting crimes of Ferdinand and Keane, *Sunday Times* columnist Rod Liddle asked: 'In the normal world, which is the greater crime?' The journalist said Keane should 'still be banged up' for his tackle on Haaland – a full four years after the offence. (There's media judgementalism for you!) What he might have argued was that Ferdinand, for his act of wrong-doing, deserved little more than a slap on the wrist.

Sport's 'war on doping' is both irrational and bound to fail

Why doping specifically should be taken more seriously than other forms of cheating in sport is not immediately apparent. Four arguments are typically advanced by drugs-busters like Dick Pound, the founding director of Wada. But, as we shall see, all have their problems.

The four, in no particular order, are: (1) Doping compels 'clean' athletes to turn 'dirty'; (2) Doping is dangerously unhealthy; (3) Doping breaches a sporting contract between athletes; and (4) Doping constitutes an unnatural interference in otherwise 'pure' competition.

Of the four arguments, the last one is the easiest to dismiss. Professional sport is far removed from a state of nature. Athletes may once have turned up for competition with little or no preparation bar everyday exercise. But today they work out using advanced technology and artificial diets. Muscles are developed not in the 'natural' course of life, through 'working the land' for example, but in the controlled environment of the weights room. No modern athlete survives without technology, whether it's shock-absorbent running shoes, 'Fastskin' swimming costumes, or graphite tennis rackets. Among the array of treatments used – quite legally – in sport are cryotherapy chambers, which are basically large refrigerators that promise to speed up recovery from fatigue in training. Doping, in this context, is just one of many forms of artificial interference in human performance.

Of argument number 3, the first thing that should be said is that it assumes athletes have an agreement with one another not to use drugs. This assumption may not always hold. In power sports such as sprinting, for example, drug use is so widespread that athletes may well have come to accept doping as part and parcel of the sport. Or perhaps there is a tacit agreement that certain forms of doping – like HGH treatments – are kosher, whereas others – like steroid use – are not.

But even if there is a consensus that drugs should not be used in sport, it's unclear as to how an athlete is 'betraying' his peers by doping any more than he would be betraying them if he committed some other sporting offence. A rugby player who carries out a deliberate spear-tackle, thus putting an opponent's life in danger, is surely guilty of a much more serious breach of covenant – namely the sacred covenant to avoid trying to kill a fellow player.

Argument 2 carries some weight, in that performance-enhancing drugs generally have unhealthy side-effects which can be dangerous and even fatal when the drugs are poorly administered. Steroids are particularly risky, commonly giving rise to behavioural disorders like mood swings – so-called 'roid rage' – and some long-term physical problems. At the same time, drug use must be compared to other, legal practices in sport that can cause physical or mental harm. Jockeys starve themselves to make racing weights. Sumo wrestlers fatten themselves for extra strength. Marathon runners risk damage to their joints by perpetual training. Compare also the number of known doping-related deaths in sport to the number of deaths and injuries from so-called ordinary play. In England, roughly two rugby players a year suffer serious spinal injuries during games. In Australia, the figure is closer to four a year. Across the globe, in rugby, there are normally one or two contact-related fatalities each year. Aside from the odd cyclist and professional wrestler, there are few deaths in the history of sport that have been directly linked to doping.

The second point that should be made is that if it's the health of athletes one has at heart, then it may be better to legalise drugs and administer them in a safe environment than to drive them underground. Part of the reason why steroids are so risky in sport is that there has never been a proper study done into their cause and effect. (Indeed, due to a paucity of research, we don't know, in truth, just how many lives are shortened or snuffed out each year by drugs in sport.)

We will take up this issue again in a moment, but first look at argument 1, which on the face of it seems like the most powerful reason for treating drugs as a special case. Tellingly, Wada, in its anti-doping code of conduct, relies heavily on this particular argument, citing 'the athletes' fundamental right to participate in doping-free sport'. Wada claims that athletes are compelled to dope in order to compete. But is this entirely true? In the first instance, there is some debate about the efficacy of many perform-ance-enhancing drugs. Respected UK cycling coach Peter Keen has mentioned, for example, the 'potentially massive placebo effect of drug use in sport'. He once commented: 'At high levels of competition a huge array of interven-tions, both illegal and legal, are used in an attempt to improve performance. Many have no direct physiological effect but could be having a dramatic effect on perform-ance via psychological mechanisms that we don't yet fully understand.' A number of studies have since shown that athletes taking placebo drugs tend to out-perform those who take nothing.

Secondly, and more importantly, there is a question as to whether 'coercion' takes place, or just 'persuasion', when doping is present in sport. Athletes are still free to choose not to use drugs, and apparently can compete at a high level while doing so. The proliferation of drugs in track and field, for example, did not stop Paula Radcliffe – an outspoken anti-doping campaigner – from continuing to complete. David Millar, the Scottish cyclist, offers further enlightenment in this regard. He was caught using drugs in 2004 and, rare for his breed, admitted that he was guilty of prior doping offences. Since serving a two-year suspension, Millar has returned to the sport as a 'drug-free crusader', apparently believing that one can compete in cycling – and compete at the highest level – without using drugs. Significantly, Millar knows the comparative advantages that drugs provide and yet, so far as we know, he is still willing to compete without them.

It's hard to make a clear judgement on such matters, as no one knows the exact level of drug use in particular sports. But if, for example, you take at face value Dick Pound's comments about professional ice hockey to the effect that roughly one third of players are on drugs – considered by the US hockey league to be a high estimation – it still means about two thirds are not on drugs. Thus, it seems that athletes are not necessarily compelled to take drugs in an environment where doping takes place. There may be a temptation. But there are temptations to offend in other respects within sport. It could be argued, for instance, that the relative leniency shown towards crimes like spear-tackling and eye-gouging tempts – and maybe even compels – rugby players to perform illegal acts of violence on the pitch.

Assuming, however, that doping is a special, or 'worse', form of cheating that requires a particularly draconian response, how do you go about implementing it? Wada has set out its stall clearly, launching a 'war on doping', incorporating more widespread testing, a disciplinary procedure that puts the onus on athletes to prove their innocence, and stiff sentences for those found guilty. Its strategy has parallels with the much-debated 'war on drugs', and allied anti-crime measures, in the United States. Zero tolerance for minor offences, mandatory sentencing, and a 'three strikes and you're out' penalty scheme are among a number of shared features. In the case of Wada's campaign, no distinction is made between drugs that have a proven performance-enhancing effect and those – like marijuana – which may actually inhibit performance. Policing authorities can convict an offender when they are 'comfortably satisfied' he or she is guilty. 'This standard of proof in all cases is greater than a mere balance of probability but less than proof beyond a reasonable doubt,' Wada explains, claiming its provisions are similar to those in professional misconduct cases. But critics argue that the framework is prone to creating miscarriages of justice. Its inflexibility means that someone could face a potentially devastating ban for doing something as little as forgetting to register an inhaler.

Neville Cox, a barrister and globetrotting sports law lecturer who has represented an Olympic gold medallist and a number of other top athletes in doping court proceedings, describes the rules as 'rabidly fascist'. If accused of doping, he says, 'under Wada rules you would have to convince them you were abducted by aliens and had this stuff forced into you in order to succeed.' He adds: 'If Wada was serious about getting rid of drugs from sport they would give a reduced sanction for people who pleaded guilty, which all court systems do.'

The current provisions, however, are staunchly defended by Pound, who took up his first full term of office in 2001 – coincidentally the same year that no-nonsense John Walters was appointed America's 'drugs tsar'. 'Doping is organized, systematic, well-financed, well-researched cheating,' Pound is fond of saying. 'This is not going to go away by holding hands and having a zen thing and going "*ommmm*".'

But can a 'war on doping' be won any more than a 'war on drugs'? From a purely practical viewpoint, warfare – or anything like it – may be the wrong way of trying to reverse certain ingrained patters of behaviour. In America today, few people believe you can tackle drugs by law enforcement measures alone. Increased drug seizures and related arrests are heralded as progress in the societal 'war on drugs' but police believe that only a small fraction of illicit substances will ever be uncovered. Drug gangs which are taken out of commission are quickly replaced by new, often more ruthless criminals. Even Walters spoke of the need to tackle demand-side issues, promising to 'help the addicted find effective treatment and remain in recovery'.

But in the world of sport, the focus remains almost entirely on supply. Wada's 75-page anti-doping code, designed as an action plan for all sporting bodies, speaks of nothing else but enforcement. Education and other such measures that could help to reduce demand are addressed in less than two pages in the report, and with the minimum of detail. And the question of why athletes turn to drugs in the first place is not mentioned at all. 'Sports bodies never enter into discussion on why people choose to use drugs,' Cox remarks. 'They won't enter into that discussion because it will inevitably involve criticism of them, and they like to pretend doping is purely a wrong engaged in by the athlete.'

It may be the case that sporting authorities don't want to openly discuss, let alone research, the effects of drugs on sporting performance for fear of encouraging greater usage. However, one can't help thinking that if athletes were properly informed about the manner in which drugs really worked they would be more careful about using them. Dr Forest Tennant, a leading authority on anabolic steroids in the US, once commented: 'Young athletes who take heavy doses of anabolic steroids for 60 to 90 days should expect to die in their 30s or 40s.' Heavily publicising this sort of message, and complementing it with a drugs advisory service for athletes, might well yield better results in terms of reducing drug use than any amount of enforcement measures.

Such educative or rehabilitative measures may also be far more cost-effective than implementing a straightforward ban. Because drugs testing is quite expensive, sporting authorities tend to concentrate their policing efforts on elite athletes. But what about the masses of competitors at lower levels of sport? Dr Tennant estimated in 1988 that as many as 1 million athletes in the US were using anabolic steroids. How many athletes today use such drugs – in the US and across the world – is anyone's guess. But what is clear is that no Wada-endorsed testing regime has come close to reaching them. So long as that continues, sporting authorities will stand accused of prioritising protecting the image of their games over the health and welfare of their athletes.

Ask yourself: Why not legalise drugs in sport? If athletes knew they could take performance-boosting substances in a safe environment they would surely keep away from the more dangerous stuff. Yes, drug-free athletes would be placed at a competitive disadvantage but what would it matter so long as there was disclosure?

Going down this route would, of course, call for a new way of looking at sports results. Record books would have to be more nuanced, detailing just what the winners and the losers respectively were taking. Under such a liberal regime, there could be a strong incentive for athletes to stay drug-free. A 'clean' image might well have a greater marketing potential. This wouldn't be guaranteed, however. The sporting public – fans and the like – would be free to interpret results for themselves. Critically, there would be no consensus on who actually 'won' a particular event. All results would be ambiguous and open to different readings. So constituted, sport would be as much a competition of ideas as a physical contest of wills. Some fans may agree with John Gray, for example, when he says, 'the best fisherman is not the one who catches the most fish but the one who enjoys fishing the most'. Others may side with Claudio Tamburrini who argues: 'If an athlete risks her health to attain victory, while others are more prudent, it is only fair that the victory goes to the former.' Some may actually agree with both professional philosophers.

Even if sport doesn't voluntarily move in this direction, it may be compelled to do so. Thanks to the proliferation of performance-enhancing drugs, many people already take sporting results with a pinch of salt. Those numbers can only increase as new technologies come on stream. 'Gene doping', for instance, has the potential to create untold ambiguities within sport. If children are 'modified' before birth to make them more athletic, should they be banned from sport? It's surely not their fault that they turned out that way. (OK, you can blame their pushy parents if you wish.) We are already in something close to a gene doping environment thanks to the proliferation of growth hormones in society at large. In particular, there has been an emerging pattern in recent years of parents giving hormones on a routine basis to their children to boost their height and general bulk. By 2004, such children were estimated to number at least 1 million in the United States. Under such circumstances, can we say that any sporting contest today – from the playground upwards – is absolutely fair?

The past decade has seen an explosion of new performance-enhancing treatments – diuretics, probenecid and erythropoietin (EPO), to name but a few. You can be sure there are countless other such substances being used today of which we are unaware. History has shown that athletes and coaches are more than a few steps ahead of the authorities. And, with this in mind, it's possible that people will look differently upon doping offences in the future. As the full extent of drug use today becomes clear, will we see 'cheats' like Ben Johnson in a new light?

More than 90 years ago, an athletic superstar was stripped of two Olympic gold medals for a breach of the rules. Jim Thorpe was banned from track and field and publicly disgraced – all because he had defied the IOC's strict 'amateurism' code by playing the occasional game of professional league baseball prior to the 1912 Summer Games. Many of his contemporaries had done the same but they were wily enough to use aliases when playing for money. The ban cast a long shadow on Thorpe's life. While he enjoyed a successful career in American football, he never quite overcame his 'outsider' tag. He struggled with alcoholism and lived out his final years as a poor man in a trailer home in California. It was another 30 years before the IOC acknowledged an error of judgement, and in 1983 Thorpe's victories were reinstated in the record books.

It's hard to imagine Johnson ever getting his gold medal back. But in 30, 60 or 90 years' time, people may well have a fresh take on the athlete, who until recently could be found living in humble circumstances at his mother's home in Toronto.

'I'm not a cheat,' said Johnson after he had been banned for life. 'I do what I am supposed to do to win.'

CHAPTER 4

BEST OF ENEMIES: SPORT, HATRED AND THE CASE OF GOLF

'No one likes us, we don't care'
> popular chant sung by Millwall FC supporters

'Hatred is by far the longest pleasure.'
> Lord Byron

'We dread them, their brown arms and rasp of money,/ their slacks the color of ice cream, their shoes,/whiter than bones, that stipple the downtrodden green/and take an open stance on the backs of the poor'
> From *Golfers*, John Updike

Sports fandom is often compared to religious belief. But it would be more accurate to compare it to the *wrong type of religious belief*. Fans are not known for their tolerance and self-discipline. Nor for 'loving your neighbour', especially when that neighbour is a Liverpool supporter and you're Man U through and through. Like religious fundamentalists whose very lifeblood is attacking people who don't share their particular faith, sports fans tend to define themselves by their opposition to 'the other'.

'I love X because I hate Y; I hate Y because I love X', is a commonly accepted equation in sport, where X equals

Glasgow Rangers, for example, and Y Glasgow Celtic. Arguably, the authentic fan is that for whom hate explicitly overtakes love as the defining sporting impulse. A fan who is recognisably wet behind the ears may start supporting, say, Manchester City because he enjoys their style of play and likes the friendly atmosphere at their home ground. But as he 'matures', his motivation for being a City fan will boil down to one thing: 'We are not United.' Or so decrees a certain, hardcore brand of fandom. In sport, as in fundamentalist religious circles, hating 'the other' is regarded as integral to authentic belief.

An illustrative discussion of this once took place on an internet website that I stumbled across. A football fan asked why people insisted on hating the opposition rather than just supporting their own team. There was a mixed response from users of the site. But, tellingly, most people took the questioner to task for his naivety. 'Oh dear. You really, really don't understand football at all, do you?' one fan remarked. 'It's an absolutely integral part of supporting any particular team that you automatically hate at least one other team … I feel rather sorry for the people who don't get that. They are missing out.' Another correspondent said: 'You can't be a real footy fan if you don't hate all the other teams.'

The view is shared by many higher up in the game. Clubs like Barcelona and Real Madrid have fostered a culture of mutual defamation, presumably to sustain interest in what is now (as we shall discuss) a largely superficial rivalry. Many clubs look jealously upon the fanatical support base of the two Spanish giants, and indeed some have tried to reproduce their formula. In the early 1990s, Costa Rica's top club Deportivo Saprissa was seeking to expand its business, and realised the best way of doing so was to create a firm of hooligans. *La Ultra Morada*, the first group of its kind in Costa Rica, emerged with the help of hooligan 'consultants' from Chilean league team Universidad de Católica. Saprissa's local rivals Alajuelense soon followed suit, developing its own hardcore fan base known as *La Doce* ('The Twelfth Man').

'The results of this investment in fanaticism were quick and spectacular,' according to soccer writer Matthew Yeomans. 'A gang culture tied to *La Ultra* and *La Doce* quickly took root, fuelled by a growing sense among poor Ticos (Costa Ricans) that the burgeoning national economy was leaving them behind. With it came a startling increase in fan violence at soccer matches and at least one death. The traditional animosity of the regular Clásico between Saprissa and Alajuelense took on new venom.'

Club directors in England have similarly wised up to the value of an insanely motivated support base. How else do you explain Delia Smith's impulsive war-cry – 'Where are you? Where are you? Let's be 'aving you!' – delivered over the public address by the celebrity chef and club shareholder during half-time at one of Norwich City's home games?

Of course, hatred in sport can't really be put in the same bracket at hatred in religion. The latter has been responsible for the loss of millions of lives down the centuries through religious wars, purges and other such catalogues of violence. The former has claimed no more than a few thousand casualties through such things as hooliganism and random pub fights. That said, it would be wrong to dismiss hatred in sport as relatively unimportant, let alone to dismiss it as the 'bit of fun' that many sports fans regard it to be.

First of all, even if you never raise a fist in anger at a rival fan, your hatred may well encourage others to do so. There is such a crime as hate-speak, and football fans are profoundly guilty of it. A 2005 BBC *Panorama* investigation of Glasgow's Old Firm rivalry estimated that each game between Celtic and Rangers left about 40 people hospitalised with stabbing injuries, 'bottled' faces and similar wounds. Such violence could not have taken place without an atmosphere of spite, as the Scottish football journalist Graham Spiers told *Panaroma*. 'You have the drama of the game itself and the atmosphere, and yes, if you ignore the specific sentiment, if you ignore the bigoted vocabulary, yes it's an exciting environment. But,' he said, 'down the nexus chain there is death at the end of it.'

Spiers' personal experience is revealing. A lifelong supporter of Rangers, he has suffered a barrage of attacks in recent years for daring to question the club's record on tackling sectarianism. Charged by die-hard Rangers fans with something akin to sporting apostasy, Spiers was subjected to a particularly bitter hate-campaign in December 2005 when the Rangers Supporters' Trust sought to have him sacked by the *Herald*, the newspaper for which he was then working. The Trust listed several supposed crimes, including Spiers' description of certain of Rangers' traditions and chants as 'offensive', and his declaration in a newspaper column that he hoped sometime to have 'a very splendid private dinner with [Martin] O'Neill', the then Celtic manager. 'The time for sitting idly by when lies and propaganda are aimed in our direction is over,' the fans declared.

The tenor of the Trust's communication, with its all-or-nothing – 'you are either with us or against us' – logic, has echoes of the sort of rhetoric associated with religious fanatics. Working themselves up into a spiteful frenzy, hardened supporters of Rangers – and indeed Celtic – display a depth of passion rarely seen outside of Taliban army training camps. Such football fans not only mimic religious fundamentalists in the tenor, and tone, of their bile, they also exploit the same technology. The internet, in particular, has become the vehicle of choice for disseminating hate-speak, whether it's directed at Godless sinners, or card-carrying Red Devils fans.

Admittedly, Celtic and Rangers is a somewhat extreme case within sport. Not all football rivalries result in death or serious injury, which prompts the question: Is hatred acceptable when the stakes are lower?

Some lessons perhaps can be learnt from the religious field, where hatred acts as a means of problem avoidance. If you are a fundamentalist Christian, the best way of guaranteeing your belief system goes unexamined is to attack everyone else over their supposed faults. In this context, hate can be seen as a profound form of self-deceit. And self-deceit is surely something that is never good, even if it extends only to believing that your football club is the 'chosen' or 'righteous' one.

• MOST DIFFERENCES WITHIN SPORT ARE SUPERFICIAL •

The above thesis holds particularly in the case of football clubs. From both a political and a moral standpoint, and perhaps even from a cultural one also, one club is very much like another. Manchester United fans like to portray their chief Merseyside rivals as dour, jobless flat-dwellers and Liverpool fans like to think of United folk as fair-weather 'prawn cocktail' digesters. Yet figures from the Barclays Premier League show that the two clubs have almost identical fan-bases in terms of their socio-economic make-up. The average income of Liverpool fans is virtually the same as that of their United counterparts. And despite suggestions that the latter are somehow more fickle, or less committed to their side, the statistics show that Liverpool has a 'younger' length of support at home fixtures. Asked how long they had been attending their club's games, 44 per cent of those surveyed at Old Trafford in the 2006/07 season stated '25 years plus' compared to 40 per cent at Anfield.

There may be some logic to certain club identities. But claims to the effect that one club is morally superior to another because of the exceptional loyalty, or sportsmanship, of its fans – or because of the commendable ethics of its management – are almost sure to be bogus. Manchester City does have a slightly higher proportion of working-class followers than Manchester United. But that makes next to no difference to the way in which the club operates. Both City and United charge similar ticket prices and both happen to be owned by foreigners. When you boil it down, about the only real difference between the two clubs – apart from the recent gulf in footballing success – is the fact that one is supported by Liam Gallagher and the other by Mick Hucknall (now, read as much into that as you like).

Internationally, the same principle applies: Clubs have far more in common than in contrast. The rivalry between Real Madrid and Barcelona attracts more verbiage perhaps than any other. Yet it's largely a historical rivalry, made redundant by the death of Real's one-time benefactor, the former Spanish dictator General Francisco Franco in 1975. Today, Real and Barça are separated by mostly superficial differences. It's true that Barcelona FC has a unique ownership structure which, in theory, gives 'ordinary fans' a voice in how the club is run. It's true also that

Barça breaks ranks with other clubs by refusing to allow a sponsor onto its jerseys, and instead *pays* the children's charity Unicef to put its logo on the attire. But, critically, Barça is not alone in making charitable gestures.

Some Barça fans believe the Unicef deal was aimed at softening up the club for a commercial shirt sponsor, citing the fact that Barcelona FC president, Joan Laporta, had been negotiating with different companies prior to the announcement. Moreover, Barça *does* allow Nike to display its 'swoosh' logo on its jerseys. In fact, a month after announcing the Unicef deal, which was to last between 2006 and 2011, the club said it had agreed a €150 million five-year sponsorship agreement with Nike. Whether the scale of the deal was influenced by the fact that the US clothing giant would have no 'competing' sponsor on Barça's jerseys is open to debate. What is certain, however, is that much of the good arising from the Unicef deal was undone by Barcelona's somewhat sanctimonious stance on the affair.

'It's an initiative with soul,' said Laporta of the charity agreement. 'It means winning the Champions League on a social level.' Evoking Barça's motto '*més que un club*', Laporta continued: 'To say that it is more than a club is to recognise that it aspires to something more than sporting success ... It represents the Catalan nation and in so doing embodies the civic, moral and democratic values of Catalunya [Catalonia], an open and inclusive society.'

Open and inclusive? Try telling that to Real Madrid's Luis Figo, who was pelted with bottles, coins, golf balls and even a pig's head when he turned up for a *clásico* game against his old side in 2002. Sponsorship deals aside, Barça has some serious questions to answer about hooliganism in its ranks. Its firm of die-hard fans, the *Boixos Nois*, or Mad Boys, are one of the most menacing football gangs in Europe, carrying a reputation worse even than Real's *Ultra Surs*.

In *How Football Explains the World*, US soccer writer Franklin Foer makes a valiant attempt to explain why Barcelona is morally superior to other football clubs (he is a Barça fan). His argument is infused with the rhetoric of Laporta, and boils down to the following (and I quote from Foer's book): 'Supporters of Barça want nothing more badly than victory, except for romance.'

Hmm?

Barça's team colours may well have been plucked from the French Revolution. But today it's a member of the European football aristocracy, wheeling and dealing like the rest of them in a far from sentimentalist manner. Barça does play a specific role as a home for Catalan nationalism but most Barça fans – the millions of non-Spanish supporters whose merchandise-buying has resulted in the club becoming the second richest in the world (after Real) – probably couldn't even identify Catalonia on a map.

The truth is that football clubs – Barça included – are largely apolitical. Laporta is a Catalan nationalist but he doesn't allow his passion for his province to influence his business decisions. Some years ago he inserted a clause in players' contracts requiring them to learn Catalan, but virtually all of his foreign stars ignored it – without any repercussions.

Naturally, the fact that a club is apolitical doesn't stop its fans from projecting various political affiliations onto it. The Chelsea 'Headhunters' bizarrely imagine their club – perhaps the most cosmopolitan outfit in the Premier League – to be some sort of bastion of white, English superiority. Despite a successful peace process in Northern Ireland, they still like to sing 'No Surrender to the IRA' at match fixtures. But, then again, their grasp of politics never seemed to be particularly good, as demonstrated by undercover television reporter Donal MacIntyre, when he infiltrated the hooligan gang for a BBC documentary in 1999. Quite farcically, MacIntyre convinced the Headhunters he was an Ulster loyalist – even though he spoke with a soft Dublin brogue. It was like watching a scene from *'Allo 'Allo!* where French café owner, René, tries to pass himself off as a German.

Certain fans within Italian soccer are similarly guilty of projecting bogus identities onto their clubs. At Inter Milan, for instance, a group of supporters with left-wing tendencies have rebranded their club as some kind of an 'anti-American' or 'anti-globalisation' movement. In *How*

Football Explains the World, Foer gives a hilarious account of an evening with a few of these Inter intellectuals who are fond of discussing the sins of Silvio Berlusconi, the Italian politician who just happens to own Inter's local rivals, AC Milan. Dressed in fashionable communista garb, the fans met Foer in a theatre basement under a framed picture of Che Guevara to debate how Inter served as a bulwark against the march of capitalism. This was despite 'certain contradictions', as Foer puts it mildly.

'First of all, it doesn't make any sense to liken the club to the anti-globalisation movement. An oil magnate owns Inter,' Foer comments. 'Then, when they try to graft cosmopolitanism onto the club, they fail miserably. They can never get past the fact that Inter represents the petite bourgeoisie of northern Italy, a group that resents immigration more than any in the country. The stands of Inter games contain far more racist chants and banners than they do for Berlusconi's club.' Exactly how open-minded Inter fans are can be seen by, for example, their targeting of AC Milan's Brazilian goalkeeper Dida with missiles during a Champions League game in 2005, and their yelling of monkey chants at Messina's Ivorian defender, Marc Zoro, in a Serie A match in 2006.

Irrational as it is to hate supporters of a rival team because they are wearing the 'wrong' colours, it is equally irrational to hate practitioners of a rival sport because, for example, they play with a different-shaped ball. This point is lost on many a sports fan who defines his authenticity by the strength of his passion both for a particular game, and against a supposedly diametrically-opposed other. Hardened soccer folk look down on 'rugger buggers'. Toughened rugby folk look down on soccer 'scum'. Yet neither position is really tenable, as Rod Liddle inadvertently reminded us in an article in *The Spectator* on the eve of the 2007 Rugby World Cup. Liddle used the occasion to air his prejudice against the oval-balled game – a prejudice towards which, incidentally, I was instinctively sympathetic, having being forced to play rugby against my will in school. Critically, however, nothing Liddle had to say in the piece could have been classified as an argument.

'The game of rugby is almost wholly devoid of … "skill"; it is a game of brute force and speed and a bit of tactical planning and that's yer lot.' (Said, incidentally, by a Millwall fan.) 'Perhaps that's why the middle classes, which have never been any good at sport, or very much else, like it so much,' Liddle continued. 'Come on: this is a sport for gay, middle-class cavemen … it's a useless game. If it were a better game, like football, more people would be interested in playing it.' And so on, for roughly 1,000 words.

To give Liddle some credit, he said 'many' of the reasons he disliked rugby were either 'irrational or a consequence of my habitual inverted snobbery'. Unfortunately he proceeded to construct a case against the game that on face value purported to be logical. In doing so, Liddle reminded us how verbalising hatred sounds exactly like clutching at straws. His article was also revealing in that it provided an insight into the mind of a sports fan who was convinced of his own authenticity. Liddle's hatred for one code (in this case rugby) fed off his proclaimed love for another. 'Call it "soccer", Liddle barked, 'and I'll kick your f****** head in. Only Americans, toffs and mentals call it "soccer".

While not condoning this sort of insanity, I can relate to it in that I once harboured a hatred as strong as Liddle's towards a sport: not rugby, but golf. For a long time, golf was to me a sporting aberration. Like City fans who grew up hating United as if to prove their loyalty, I advanced in years despising golf and believed that my spite showed me up to be a more genuine fan – of football in particular. Football was good, golf was evil. This simple equation went unchallenged in my mind. And I liked it that way. Hating golf gave me a terrific feeling of moral superiority. Mine was The People's Game. Theirs was a rich man's folly, or, in the words of Orwell, 'an inherently snobbish game ... which causes whole stretches of the countryside to be turned into carefully guarded class preserves'.

The only problem was that the more I thought about it, the more I realised that placing golf on a different ethical plane to all other sports wasn't really tenable. Why, for example, should soccer (get over it, Rod) be called The People's Game when it's controlled by a bunch of billionaire tycoons and run largely along feudal lines? And why should golf be seen as a game for stuck-up nobs when

137

quite a few ordinary, working-class people play it – without necessarily developing obnoxious political views (I emphasise 'necessarily')?

FANS TEND TO DEMONISE 'THE OTHER' SO THEY CAN DEFLECT ATTENTION FROM THEIR OWN FAULTS, AND FROM PROBLEMS INHERENT TO THEIR TEAM OR PREFERRED SPORT

Not wanting to let golf completely off the hook, you could argue that golf is a game through which the sins of sport shine brightest. All sporting codes have elitism, arrogance, a sanctimonious air and some dodgy lines of clothing. But, in every respect, none quite matches golf. So runs a particular line of thought, which – I must admit – still appeals to me. One of the most annoying aspects of golf is the way in which it claims to be 'cleaner' than all others.

In the fawning words of *Sports Illustrated* columnist Rick Arnett, golf 'is the most honest and thus, best, of all' games. 'Compared to the other sports, golf is bleach-white clean … Next time your favourite pro athlete's urine specimen tests out like a bio-hazard or an appalling call costs your team a victory, be thankful at least one professional sport still soars above the muck.' With rules covering every possible eventuality on the course, golf purports to have created a system of perfect justice – a system supposedly unattained by rival pursuits. In truth, however, golf – like every other game – has its cheats and if John Updike is to be believed, it has a disproportionate number of them. 'Just how childlike golf players become is proven by their frequent inability to count past five,' the author (and golfer) once remarked. Golf even has its doping cheats, although the sport seems to be in a state of denial about them. In 2007, an Italian professional golfer tested positive for a banned substance – just days after the sport's bosses rubbished claims by retired pro Gary Player to the effect that at least ten top players were using human growth hormone, creatine or steroids.

The problem here isn't cheating (needless to say, all sports have cheating). It's the emphatic, self-righteous denial of cheating by the golfing establishment – a denial that is all the more hypocritical when one considers how players in the sport are allowed to get an unfair advantage over one another through the purchase of restricted-access technology. Yes, yes – before golfing readers jump in – I know money can help you to buy success in all sports. But in no sport is the relationship between money and individual success so symbiotic – and measurably so – as in golf. Golf clubs, golf balls and even golf shoes come with distinct selling-points: the promise usually of a few extra yards on your tee-shot, or an extra bit of accuracy with your putting. That mightn't seem like much. But, as golfers will confirm, theirs is a game of inches. Moreover, the sport is quite aware of how the playing field can be unlevelled by financial expenditure. It's common for golf retailers to brag about their products' 'yard-stealing' features. 'It'll almost feel like cheating,' screams the US supplier of a technological gizmo that helps you to judge the distances between your ball and the pin.

I dislike golf too because of its overt elitism. Golf is a rich man's game – to the top of which some not-so-rich people have occasionally risen. The fact that the world's number one, Tiger Woods, comes from beyond golf's white-skinned, upper-class roots is not proof of golf's accessibility. It's proof of the reverse. Were people of all ethnic groups and economic backgrounds able to compete on an equal basis in the game, you would expect at least one Nigerian, for instance, in the world's Top 100. Instead, not a single African makes that list – with the exception of a few South African whites. At the end of October 2007, 42 of the top 100-ranked players in the world were American, ten were from Britain and Ireland, ten from Australia, ten from Nordic countries, and eight from (the white part of) South Africa. The remaining players were drawn from less than a dozen other countries. Just one, Vijay Singh – a Fijian of Indian ancestry – hailed from a background of relative poverty.

It's perhaps no coincidence that Singh, something of a self-made man, has had a particularly uneasy relationship with the golfing establishment. The sort of minority which pro-golf seems to prefer is a player who is born with a silver spoon in his mouth. The Americanised son of a wealthy international businessman usually fits the bill.

As for golf's biggest international event, a contest comprising 24 men from two continents, the Ryder Cup is a clear statement of how golf views the rest of the world: *Asia, Africa, South America … you don't really exist.*

Golfers counter this claim of elitism with the suggestion that more people have access to the sport than ever before. They point to the increased number of public golf courses where anyone with a set of clubs can play a round for a modest fee. It's not quite 'sport for all' but it's 'sport for a rising number of Ordinary Joes', they say. What such golfers really mean, however, is that people who have less money than they have are free to hack around a crappy, council-run facility until they develop the right contacts and jump through the requisite hoops in order to get into a proper club.

If you are confined to playing on public courses you *know* you are playing a different game to your fortunate fellow citizens tucked up in the Royal Saint Judas' Golf and Country Club Links. The sport operates a calculated system of apartheid, whereby one group of players is strictly kept apart from another – for socio-economic reasons that are often tied up with race and gender issues. To their shame, many aspiring members of Saint Judas', or its equivalent, are happy to wait outside the gates under the illusion that they are equals in some kind of meritocracy.

Admittedly, some 'putting peasants' are acutely aware of the stratified nature of their sport. They enjoy golf and – to their credit – they are determined not to let their toffee-nosed neighbours stop them from playing. They argue that playing golf is the best way of changing the sport – and, in this, they could be right. If the golf courses of the world become flooded with ordinary people – and if the leader-boards of international tournaments become populated with non-Americans and non-Europeans – the sport's current hierarchy would almost certainly abandon the game for some more elitist pursuit. This, after all, is the history of sport. Members of the upper classes played soccer until it became too common. They went skiing until working-class folk started turning up in large numbers on package holidays in Andorra. Golf is perhaps the next battleground between castes, and already the ridiculously rich, eager to prove their 'natural' pre-eminence, are eyeing alternatives to the game. In oil-rich Gulf states, a new craze among young playboys is point-to-point desert racing in expensive 4x4s. Over time, ever-more-exclusive games will doubtlessly be invented. The likes of jet-ski polo and moon golf are probably just around the corner. What odds on human hunting before the end of the century?

Ultimately, then, I've come to the conclusion that golf is elitist but only relatively so. It's not uniquely elitist from a sporting perspective. Nor is it uniquely hypocritical with regards to cheating and related issues. Yes, those US pro golfers who parade their Christianity on the fairway, splattering 'WWJD' ('What Would Jesus Do?') stickers on their golf bags, are hugely irritating. (As if Jesus would be seen dead on a golf course.) But there's something incongruous too about those contracted professional footballers who wear 'I belong to Jesus' T-shirts. Or indeed about those rugby players who bless themselves theatrically and blow kisses to the heavens, in between bouts of inflicting physical pain on their opponents.

It goes without saying that any sport loved by Donald Trump, Ant and Dec, and the Burmese junta needs to be treated with the highest suspicion. And, yes, it *is* grating the way in which playing golf is virtually obligatory in certain corporate circles. But, then, the latter has much to do with the prominent role of sport generally in social relations. If golf didn't exist, ambitious young stockbrokers would play against their bosses (and strategically lose to them) in, say, ping-pong, athletics or bowling. And, if there was never another PGA tournament shown on TV, the small-talk at business lunches would simply turn to Formula 1.

If I'm being completely honest with myself, the irrational, over-the-top emotions that I once harboured against golf were rooted in something closely akin to jealousy. I used to see, or read about, all those tycoons and Masters of the Universe playing rounds with one another, and I would resent the fact that they were enjoying themselves. What's more, they were enjoying themselves without me.

I accept now that people of wealth are entitled to their recreational outlets. It's not golf's fault that a certain class of slimeball social-climber is habitually drawn towards the game. Moreover, it's not the fault of golf *per se* that different social strata exist. It's true that Donald Trump never invited me on a fourball at one of his private courses. But, then, Robbie Williams never called me for a five-a-side on the AstroTurf pitch in his back garden, and I didn't once blame football for that.

The bottom line is that you can play golf without being a smug, self-centred prat, and you can be a smug self-centred prat without playing golf. Or so I have come to accept – after much soul-searching and with a heavy heart, I emphasise. In this respect, there may be a valuable lesson from my experience. To those other people in sport who hate a particular team, a particular game, a particular player, or some other specific entity – maybe a commentator (take your pick there), I'll say this: Hating is fun but letting it go is enlightening.

CHAPTER 5

REDTOPS RULE: SPORT, LIES AND SELF-DECEIT

'What luck for the rulers that the people do not think.'
Adolf Hitler

'Hitler has compelled humanity to accept a new categorical imperative: orient your thinking and acting so that Auschwitz would never repeat itself, so that nothing similar would recur.'
Theodor Adorno, philosopher

'LET'S BLITZ FRITZ'
headline in the *Sun* ahead of England's Euro '96 game against Germany

Sports journalists weren't entirely to blame for the media farce that was Bob Woolmer's 'murder'. But it's hard to imagine how it would have happened without them. It was they who largely 'broke' the story – as the first members of the international press corps on site at the Cricket World Cup in the Caribbean, where Woolmer's body was found; they who gave the story legs (and arms and hands and a head with a turban on top); they who turned half-baked theories into facts; they who gave unnamed fantasist sources unlimited publicity; they who ignored contradictions in the 'murder' tale from the outset (believing the truth should never get in the way of a good yarn); and they who – most farcically of all – put all the blame on the Jamaican police, and the Jamaican press, for giving them a bum-steer after it turned out that Woolmer died, as had initially been thought, of natural causes.

The fiasco was entirely predictable. Send a group of cricket hacks who – no offence, but – have never had to write a genuine news story since they were cub reporters off to a tropical resort. Ply them with drink and have them cover a match every second day over the course of two months. Get an editor to harangue them about the need to justify an expensive jolly with a flow of exciting copy. And you are almost guaranteed to end up with some-thing like the tale of cricket coach Woolmer's murder at the hands of Pakistani sports fanatics ... or – depending on the media outlet – match-fixing mobsters, disgruntled professional cricketers and/or a deadly venomous snake that sneaked into Woolmer's hotel room.

Sports journalists have no monopoly on inaccurate reporting. But their craft is particularly steeped in decep-tion. Take the reporting of transfer gossip, or rumours surrounding contract negotiations between players and their clubs. Such 'information' is known as gossip for a reason: it is unreliable, having often been disseminated by players' agents, or other persons with a vested interest in spreading lies. Yet the same information appears daily in pages of reputable broadsheets, masquerading – so far as anyone can tell – as news. In one week alone in the summer of 2007, I read that West Ham's then top striker, Carlos Tevez, would be leaving the club for both Inter Milan and Real Madrid, as well as seeing through his three-year contract at Upton Park. (In the end, Manchester United swooped for him.)

Some tales of gossip develop a life of their own, becoming 'news stories' that run for days on end – before disappearing into the ether as suddenly as they had arrived. One of the biggest sports stories in the US in 2006 was the reported departure of New York Yankees manager Joe Torre from the club which he had led to four World Series titles. The *Daily News* scooped the nation when it ran a front-page headline 'Outta Here!' next to a picture of the legendary coach. The only problem was that the quote was fabricated, and so was the story. Torre spent a full week denying the reports but this only added to the media frenzy. Eventually, he summoned the entire press pack to a media conference at which he issued yet another denial – and this, finally, did the trick. The assembled hacks skulked away in search of another fantasy, leaving 'all concerned looking downright silly by the time the smoke cleared', in the words of one US sports scribe.

In fairness to sports journalism, it's suffering from a malaise characteristic to all media – one described thus by former *Independent on Sunday* editor, Ian Jack: 'Today a spectre haunts the editorial floor – the spectre of the reader's boredom, the viewer's lassitude. If customers are to stay with the product, they need, or are thought to need, a diet of surprise, pace, cuts-to-the-chase, playfulness, provocation, drama, "human interests". Everything but the truth, he might have added.

One noteworthy trend has been the disappearance, or downgrading, of 'correction and clarification' columns in the print media. Media outlets which highlight errors they have made, presumably on the basis that it will build up trust with their readers, are seen as vaguely old-fashioned and quite possibly heading for extinction. In place of the ancient dictum 'facts are sacred', is an unwritten principle that newspapers can play fast and loose with the truth on the grounds that readers believe that everything is being spun, subjectivised, or sexed-up anyway.

Because of its inherently 'playful' nature, sport has featured prominently in this revolution in media values. It has been given an elevated standing in news coverage, and in recent years has arguably drawn resources away from serious (read 'boring') areas of reportage such as politics and world news. Thirty years ago, the benchmark for investigative reporting was Bernstein and Woodward of Watergate fame. Today it's 'The Fake Sheikh' Mazher Mahmood who tries to entrap figures like former England manager Sven-Goran Eriksson and Newcastle FC chairman Freddie Shepherd into confessing misdemeanours of questionable significance.

SPORTS JOURNALISM OFTEN MORE CLOSELY RESEMBLES ADVERTISING RATHER THAN NEWS

Are standards of journalism worse in sport than in other fields of reportage? Leaving aside the Woolmer fiasco (which, in fairness, was a collective cock-up involving both sports journalists and their news colleagues and editors who, to a large degree, pushed the flimsy murder theory), is there anything to say that sports journalists are particularly slovenly, unprofessional or careless about facts? One might argue the reverse, in that such journalists have an extremely discerning audience. To the average fan, a scribe's credibility can be permanently destroyed by, for example, naming David Beckham's first club as a trialist as Manchester United rather than Leyton Orient. To statistics-obsessed football supporters who digest facts and figures as a hobby, an error on behalf of a *paid* commentator is practically unforgivable.

Nonetheless, sports journalists do have serious questions to answer in relation to editorial independence. Like motoring correspondents who are generally pro-car, and property writers who are generally pro-development, sports hacks are generally pro-sport. It's a rare golfing correspondent who will investigate alleged racism or sexism in the game, and a rare racing correspondent who will ask thorny questions about animal cruelty.

This is not just a reflection on the character of media personnel. It's also a reflection of the environment in which they operate. Sports organisations are notoriously sensitive to criticism. Dare to identify wrongdoing in the Church of Soccer, Athletics or Swimming and you can expect a cover-up and a closing of ranks of which the Vatican would be proud. Make too much of a nuisance of yourself and you could be blackballed for months, years, or perhaps even an entire career.

Manchester United has attracted a number of complaints from journalists in this regard, with some reporters claiming that they have been barred from Old Trafford for asking awkward questions (i.e. for doing their jobs). Even mild-manned John 'Motty' Motson once got the 'hairdryer' treatment from United boss Alex Ferguson – for asking a relatively innocuous question about Roy Keane's disciplinary record. 'You've no right to ask that question, you're out of order, you know full well my ruling on that,' fumed Ferguson. The United manager summed up his attitude to the media in an interview with the *Daily Mail* before the start of the 2007/08 Premier League season. 'My job is to keep us out of the press,' he said. 'That's my biggest job. That's why I give you lot nothing.'

With such feelings prevalent in the club, Manchester United has done the logical thing and created its own media platform – MUTV – through which all 'news' at the club is conveyed. Naturally enough, MUTV has imported the sort of journalistic values once found on Soviet state television, routinely censoring any potentially embarrassing stories, like Keane's notorious diatribe against his under-performing team-mates in 2005. Condemning what he perceived to be a lack of commitment from his colleagues, the Irishman told striker Ruud van Nistelrooy to stop 'fiddling' with his hair to look good in front of the cameras, and instead concentrate on scoring goals. Or so we understand from leaked reports. The interview was spiked by the club and has never been aired.

That a company like Manchester United would seek to manage its public image is not surprising. What *is* surprising is that there is little obvious resistance from a supposedly independent media. In the political or financial world, a company that puts the squeeze on journalists probing for the truth would generally be met with retaliatory outrage. Despite competitive pressures, different media outlets tend to unite as one when a messenger comes under fire. However, in the sporting world, there appears to be no honour among hacks. If you get frozen out by some sporting franchise or athlete, then tough! Your peers may actually celebrate as they now have one less scribe to worry about.

Consider the experience of Andrew Jennings, an investigative reporter who has been writing periodically for the *Daily Mail* about shady dealings in Fifa. He claims to have been banned from numerous press conferences held by the world football governing body, and he has been seen on BBC's *Panorama* trying without success to get answers from senior Fifa officials, including Sepp Blatter, about alleged vote-rigging and corruption within the organisation. Significantly, there has been no major protest from the rest of the press corps about Jennings' treatment. Some hacks have asked questions on his behalf at press conferences but most have avoided causing a fuss. Or so Jennings reports in his book, *Foul! The Secret World of Fifa*. Describing the atmosphere surrounding Blatter's re-election as president of Fifa in 2002, he writes: 'Sports reporters watched the footie, retyped Blatter's press releases, merrily pressed SEND and repaired to the pub.'

Of course, media self-censorship can be found in other fields too. Tony Blair notoriously used to play journalists off each other, inviting only a select (and inevitably loyal) few into his inner circle. But, notwithstanding all his disagreements with the BBC over its coverage of Britain's decision to go to war in Iraq, the former prime minister never went so far as to cut off all ties with the Beeb – which is more than can be said for Ferguson. The United boss has given the public service broadcaster the cold shoulder since it aired a controversial TV documentary on his agent son, Jason, in 2004. In September 2007, Ferguson said he planned never to speak to the BBC again.

PROFESSIONAL SPORT IS INDISTINGUISHABLE FROM THE HYPE SURROUNDING IT

The lack of professional loyalty shown by sports media outlets to one another is perhaps partly a reflection of their collective independence – or rather non-independence. Newspaper and broadcast media are not just observers in the world of sports, they are players. Tune into the

BBC during Wimbledon, for example, and you will never hear Sue Barker declare: 'This afternoon we have got a really pedestrian contest. A 41st seed going up against a 23rd seed. Eminently missable stuff.' No, the job of a broadcaster is to keep people watching whatever sporting event it is that you happen to have exclusive broadcasting rights over. Some marketing techniques are subtle – such as BSkyB's promotion of Premier League fixtures on its news bulletins. Other techniques are not-so-subtle, and into this category falls the following example from Sky Sports presenter Richard Keys. In December 2005, with Chelsea in a virtually unassailable position at the top of the Premiership table, Keys struggled to find a reason for viewers to stay tuned to the league. '[Manchester] United have got two games this week that could get them to within seven points of Chelsea. The champions play Arsenal next weekend, and if they lost that and United kept on winning, the gap would be four points and then it would be game on,' he panted.

As it turned out, United lost their next game and Chelsea widened their lead to eighteen points, thus helping them to wrap the title up with ease.

One might have thought that sports fans would feel a little insulted by the way in which they are patronised by the media. But viewing figures show that promotional bumf is almost as important to spectators as the fixture which it surrounds. The most watched TV programme in Australia each year is usually the Aussie Rules Grand

Final, with an audience of roughly 3 million. However, the post-match analysis broadcast (with a typical audience of 2.5 million) comes not far behind. Nor, indeed, does the pre-match build-up show (with a typical audience of 2.25 million). Many a fan of English soccer will be able to relate to such viewing patterns. I can recall frequently sitting through three hours of the BBC's slick build-up coverage to an FA Cup Final only to quit watching the match somewhere into the first half.

Fans, it seems, have bought into the thinking that you can't have enough noise around a sporting contest; you can't have enough previewing, reviewing, analysing, debating, discussing, parodying, post-morteming. But, ask yourself, what were the most memorable sporting events of your life? Were they televised? Were they headline acts? Or were they rather episodes of a much more personal, localised nature? When people were asked to recall their favourite moments involving George Best, around the time of the footballer's death, it is perhaps telling that many cited obscure matches at backwater clubs that 'ne'er deigned *Match of the Day*'. As though the glamour of Best's brace against Benfica in the 1966 European Cup quarter-final, and his six goals against Northampton Town in 1970, had been diminished through over-exposure, fans waxed lyrical instead about games which they themselves attended – games from which there was little, if any, surviving television footage. One such match was Chelsea vs. Manchester United in September 1964, a game in which the eighteen-year-old Best scored one goal and set up a second. A rare witness to the event poignantly recalled: 'It was a downpayment on legend.'

Significantly, in the days before video technology and mobile phone clips, fans could travel to a match knowing that they might witness something unique, or perhaps discover a one-in-a-million like Best. Today, however, if you saw 'the next Best' at Stamford Bridge the whole world would know about it almost simultaneously. By the time you had got to Fulham Broadway to catch the underground home, perhaps some of your mates would be downloading the action on YouTube – and where lies your 'discovery' then? A further effect of the omnipresence of video is that sport fans (to their loss) tend to undervalue events that go unrecorded on film. If a goal can't be found in the vaults of the BBC's cuttings department then it never really happened. So, at least, we have come to believe. Commenting on the way in which football memories are skewed by technology, the broadcaster Michael Parkinson once said: 'The trouble with nostalgia is that it starts with the invention of video tape. Everything that went before is left to old men on park benches and grand-dads telling stories ... "The 100 Best Goals Ever Scored" is a misnomer. It is, in fact, "The 100 Best Goals Ever Seen on Television", a different proposition altogether.'

It's fair to say that some sporting events would never have registered in the public consciousness were it not for TV and other such media. Bob Beamon's record jump in the 1968 Mexico City Olympics became an event of legendary proportions largely because of Tony Duffy's iconic photograph of the athlete suspended in mid-air. Some other events, however, have benefited from the absence of concrete records. One of the most famous underdog victories in rugby union history was Irish provincial side Munster's defeat of the touring All Blacks in 1978. The event has spawned no end of urban myths, as well as a hugely successful play, *Alone It Stands*. But would the Thomond Park game have the same mystique if there was TV footage available of it?

The beauty of an unrecorded episode is that the few spectators who witness it can shape it into something poetic without fear of contradiction. Had television been around in the late 19th century, the American author Richard Harding Davis could not have penned the following, epic lines about a Yale–Princeton football game that he had witnessed:

> The Yale men had forced the ball to within two yards of Princeton's goal, and they had still one more chance left them to rush it across the line. While they were lining up for that effort the cheering died away, yells, both measured and inarticulate, stopped, and the place was so still that for the first time during the day you could hear the telegraph instruments chirping like crickets from the side line ... And then ... Captain Thorne made his

run, and settled the question forever. It is not possible to describe that run. It would be as easy to explain how a snake disappears through the grass, or an eel slips from your fingers, or to say how a flash of linked lightning wriggles across the sky.

Turn now to events that have been excessively hyped, or subjected to inordinate levels of media coverage. Do you remember them fondly? Do you remember them at all? Many sports are edging towards a realm currently occupied by professional wrestling, a celebration of the superficial and inauthentic in the extreme. Boxing, once a sport for athletic purists, is almost there – what with all the highly expedient trash-talk of its participants. In one of the most hyped contests of 2006, Ricardo Mayorga described Oscar De La Hoya as a 'clown' and 'an old lady that's past her prime that should be sitting home in a rocking chair doing nothing'. After being floored in the contest in the first round, and knocked out in the sixth, Mayorga said: 'You are a great champion ... I apologise for everything I said to you.' 'I forgive you,' De La Hoya replied, and they walked away collectively about $10 million richer.

There is some evidence of a contemporary backlash against hyperbole in sport. Horseracing commentator Ted Walsh recently remarked: 'All sports are being analysed far too much by bollixes like us.' Nonetheless, it's hard to see the current trend being reversed in sports coverage. Lying, either to oneself or else to others, has become ingrained in the behaviour of sporting folk – be they journalists, administrators, athletes, promoters or fans. Half-truths, quarter-truths, and complete untruths abound in the sporting world. While too numerous to mention, a few lies – or rather meta-lies – do stand out. They include:

Lie # 1. Sport is competitive:

One of the most abused phrases in the English language today is surely 'World Cup'. To suggest, for example, that a tournament comprising thirteen past or present British colonies, and the Netherlands, is representative of the international community is grossly misleading, not to say a tad Anglocentric. But the International Cricket Council got away with it, and without any protest, in 2007. Not only that, but the organisation claimed, again without apparent dissent, that its 'World Cup' represented the purest of competitive action – even though everyone pretty much knew Australia would win it.

Yes, international cricket is competitive. But only in the sense that a hypothetical military conflict between the United States and the Federal States of Micronesia is competitive. In cricket, as in other sports, a few nations tend to run the show. Surprise results are rare and becoming rarer – in part, it seems, because of professionalism and its knock-on effect on traditional competitive advantages. Within nations, professionalism has similarly tended to reduce the pool of success. The English Premier League is typically described as one of the most competitive leagues in the world. But only four teams have ever won it since its inception in 1992 (when it became known as the Premiership) – a poor return compared to its predecessor, the less commercialised First Division.

Lie # 2. Sport is entertaining:

What about this for a sporting lie: On the eve of the 2006 Fifa World Cup, one of the main team sponsors, Nike, published a footballing 'manifesto' pledging its signatories to what it called 'the beautiful game'. 'We believe that diving is for the swimming pool and arguing for politicians,' said Cristiano Ronaldo, who was widely accused of using 'simulation' tactics during the tournament. Thierry Henry, who won his team passage to the final thanks to a highly dubious penalty in the semis, was another signatory to the manifesto, as was Wayne Rooney, who got sent off in England's final match amid some proverbial 'handbags' with the aforementioned dramatist, Ronaldo.

The myth exists that sport is a celebration of the aesthetic; that it rewards beauty and entertainment instead of crude practicality. In truth, sport has little tolerance for élan – and that tolerance declines the higher up the ranks you go. In heavily commercialised sports, risk-takers are not applauded but rather scolded for 'irresponsibility'. When Robert Pires fluffed an audacious two-man penalty kick in a Premiership game in October 2005 some sympathetic applause might have been due. Instead, the Frenchman was castigated for a 'moment of madness', his sin having been to cock-up a pass to his team-mate Henry in the box, having tried to imitate a famous Johan Cruyff penalty for Ajax in 1982. The *Guardian* described the stunt as 'a dumb thing to do' – even though Pires' team were leading at the time and went on to win the game. It may have been just a coincidence, but Pires' career went into virtual free fall afterwards.

Some firmly believe that sport was more entertaining in days of yore – and they may be right. Fifty years ago, the stakes were not quite as high and the prize money not quite as great and, as a result, athletes may have had more freedom to express themselves. Golf writer Kevin Mitchell cites a new wave of conservatism in his sport – specifically as a result of increased prize money for down-the-table finishers in pro tournaments. Because of the extra rewards, he says, golfers end up 'seriously well paid for being no better, mostly, than competent'. Similar nostalgics can be found in cricket, with some fans tracing a turning point within the game to a specific Test match in 1981. New Zealand needed a six off the last ball to secure a rare victory over Australia but they were denied a shot at glory when the Australian captain, Greg Chappell, instructed his brother Trevor to bowl an underarm 'grubber' along the grass. This act of gamesmanship, with its 'professional' quality, is all too familiar to spectators today. Just as golfers 'play the percentages' rather than go for broke, footballers whose teams hold a slender lead tend to wind down the clock instead of going for goal.

One wonders in this regard how the likes of Pelé would have coped in today's footballing environment. Perhaps his most audacious stunt of all time was that dummy performed on Uruguay's goalkeeper in the 1970 World Cup. For those who can't picture the episode: Pelé was running through to collect a pass at the edge of the box and instead of taking the easy option and tapping the ball away from the goalkeeper to line up an almost certain score, the Brazilian performed a dramatic body-swerve leaving, his opponent rooted to the spot and, effectively, taken out of play. Pelé then collected the ball and fired a shot across the mouth of the goal … and wide. It was a miss but a wonderful, spectacular miss. Now, imagine him doing the same thing playing for Chelsea while José Mourinho was manager in, say, a situation where the team went on to lose. He would probably have been dropped to the reserves and docked a month's wages.

Admittedly, there is a temptation to romanticise the past. It seems that footballers with individualistic, silky skills have always been viewed with a degree of suspicion by their employers. As David Winner notes, the precociously talented Jimmy Greaves – the proverbial show pony of his day – was left out of the 1966 World Cup Final for 'workhorse Roger Hunt'. Winner goes on to argue that England managers in the 1970s treated flair as though it were 'a form of leprosy'. Thus, if today's footballers act in a cynical fashion, they do so only by degree. Soccer has always been about results. Entertainment has always given way to a 0–0 draw if it suits both sides.

'Aha!' replies the football aficionado. 'But 0–0 results can be entertaining. Give me a 90-minute, one-shot-on-goal, chess-like stalemate rather than a 5–0 drubbing any day!'

Oh, really?

Here's an exercise: Name the most boring moment of your life. Personally speaking, I've been to some extremely dodgy theatrical plays. I've put up with some hellishly dull dinner parties. But time has never dragged the way it did when I was watching Barcelona play out a coolly efficient 1–0 La Liga victory at the Nou Camp a few years ago – courtesy of (what a surprise!) a dubious penalty. This brings us nicely onto:

Lie # 3: Sport is atmospheric:

I've been to a few big sporting events in my day, and almost without exception I've been sold a lie. Cheltenham is not 'great craic', as is claimed by every tanked-up bloke who heads to the English racing festival each March. It is, in fact, a painful marathon of pushing, shoving, queuing, drinking and attempting in between to catch a glimpse of some horses. The event is best watched at home – unless your idea of fun is jostling in the toilets with burly, drunk men who keep missing the urinals and piddling on your shoes.

Football? My own infatuation for West Ham grew exponentially in 1991 when I watched the club play Nottingham Forest in a FA Cup semi-final at which Hammers' fans reacted to some misfortune in the game by spending almost the entire second half chanting uninterruptedly, 'Billy Bonds' claret and blue army'. West Ham lost the game 4–0. But they won me over. In hindsight, however, the mood at Villa Park that afternoon wasn't exactly representative of the average West Ham fixture. While Upton Park, the club's home ground, is rightly described as one of the most atmospheric – and perhaps even intimidating – grounds in England, it's quite often charged with about as much electricity as a pocket torch.

This is not to say that sporting amphitheatres are particularly un-atmospheric. But the atmosphere is often either overstated by the media, or artificially sustained. Song sheets are now handed out at many international grounds, an unheard-of practice in bygone years. In another atmosphere-boosting ploy, sports stadiums are being rebranded with names like 'Theatre of Dreams' (Manchester United), or 'House of Pain' (the Highlanders rugby club of New Zealand). Cardiff's Millennium Stadium was dubbed on its opening a 'Coliseum' and a 'Bear Pit'. A notable fad, in this regard, is to call any venue capable of putting on evening games 'The Stadium of Light', whereas just 'a stadium with floodlights' would be more apt.

As for my own national stadium for soccer and rugby in Ireland, I can safely say that 'the Lansdowne roar' has always been overrated. As a schoolboy rugby fan, I do remember a sort of wild, banshee-like yelping that rose up from time to time on the terraces. Yes, there was once a strain of uninhibited madness in the air – a madness that perhaps had its swansong in 1993 when Mick Galwey scored a try to beat England and a middle-aged woman, carrying what seemed to her shopping, hopped over the advertising hoardings to give Galwey a celebratory pat on the back. Nowadays, Irish internationals – be they at Lansdowne Road or Croke Park – attract an altogether more civilised following. The bag ladies are gone and instead beautiful young things pout in their seats, hoping to attract a cameraman so they can wave to their mates down in Oz.

Lie # 4: Sport is sentimental:

Tradition is valued in serious sport but only as a means to victory. Or, to making money. In an arena where winning is all, everything has its price. Age-old institutions like sports clubs are sold off like junk bonds. In the US, the Cleveland Browns – one of the country's most prestigious American football outfits – were shifted off to Baltimore as part of an expansion programme. In England, West Ham were flogged to a consortium that included a Spurs supporter (in former chairman Eggert Magnusson) on the promise of more silverware.

Football fans delude themselves into thinking the game is run both for them, and by them. But the latter is plainly false, while the former is true only to the extent that financial pyramid schemes are run for savers. 'In some ways I admire football fans,' Crystal Palace owner Simon Jordan once said. 'In what other business can you serve up crap and have people come back for more?'

By making loyalty a badge of identity, sports supporters are setting themselves up for exploitation. As Jordan implies, football clubs can pretty much do as they like. And the same goes for governing bodies in sport, which today less resemble 'servants of the people' than downright spoilsports. In the US, the governing body in charge of baseball recently went to the courts to try to block fans from operating 'fantasy leagues' – out of which Major League Baseball, coincidentally, wasn't making any money. The organisation argued that all data relating to its games, including statistics on batting and fielding, was copyrighted and couldn't be reproduced in any form without prior permission from the league. The league lost the case but appealed the following year.

2006 saw Fifa launching yet another purge against fans who brought 'unauthorised' merchandise into World Cup stadiums. More than 1,000 Dutch supporters were ordered to strip before the Netherlands–Ivory Coast game – just because they were wearing orange lederhosen that bore the brand name of an unofficial sponsor. And in Britain, in 2007, the FA outlawed a convention among Chelsea fans to throw celery onto the pitch while singing a somewhat obscene traditional ditty at the start of matches. The FA suggested that celery-throwing was dangerous but, really, one suspects that had there been money in the craze, the Association would simply have introduced its own 'FA-authorised' vegetables instead.

The only surprise about such killjoy behaviour on the part of governing bodies is that it surprises anyone. Each time a sporting organisation flogs to pay-per-view TV the broadcasting rights for some event that used to be shown on free-to-air, fans – and often politicians too – rise in protest. 'How can you take away our games?' they cry. 'Since when were they *your* games?' the money men reply. Trevor Phillips, chief executive of South Africa's Premier Soccer League, which was at the centre of an all-too-familiar row in 2007 about the selling of broadcasting rights for its fixtures to a private firm, spelt out the situation clearly for spectators. Asked about the league's 'social responsibilities', he replied: 'We play football for money. That is what we do.'

Some fans have taken a stand against what they see as unscrupulous behaviour by sporting bosses. When Wimbledon FC moved to Milton Keynes in 2002, for instance, a group of the club's supporters set up the London-based AFC Wimbledon in its place. In another example of 'fan power', a football journalist called Will Brooks recently established myfootballclub.co.uk with the aim of giving people a stake in their own club for just £35.

In November 2007, the website agreed to buy non-league outfit Ebbsfleet United, promising the site's 20,000 subscribers a say in team selections, transfers and all major decisions at the club. Such initiatives may be honourable but one wonders, ultimately, whether they will catch on. When it comes to a choice between glamour, on the one hand, and control over a club on the other, most fans seems to opt for the former. AFC Wimbledon may be one of the best-supported non-league clubs around, but average home attendances have fallen by 17 per cent since its inception.

For most fans, attitudes are simply hardening. Feeling unloved and taken advantage of, soccer supporters are reappraising their relationship with their 'treasured' clubs. They now see themselves less as foot soldiers in an army of claret-and-blue, or any other colour, than as consumers of a straightforward leisure product (with consumers' rights). In this regard, fans are becoming increasingly disloyal to their teams. In football, the norm today is to cheer when you are winning and whinge when you are losing. A couple of bad results is enough for a crowd to start baying for the manager's blood.

Some see this as progress. But, really, it's a question of fans being reduced to the same level as their (exploitative) clubs – of the oppressed becoming the oppressor. The assumption today is that everything – tradition, history, a sense of community, 'old-fashioned' values, etc. – can legitimately be sacrificed on the altar of sporting success. Note, for example, how little outcry there is in clubs over the demolition of memory-filled stadiums. Or, indeed, over 'foreign' takeovers. When the American sports mogul Malcolm Glazer sought to buy Manchester United – or what he touchingly called a 'great franchise' – in May 2005, the fan-led lobby group Shareholders United vowed mass demonstrations. The group predicted that up to 20,000 fans would leave the club. As an initial show of strength, it organised a mass boycott of United's match against West Bromwich Albion. Only no one stayed away. The game was a 67,000-seat sell-out.

Lie # 5: Sport makes you happy:

It's a rare sports fan who will admit to being euphoric about his obsession. According to the etiquette of die-hard fandom, a miserable visage is proof of your dedication, whereas unrestrained merriment prompts suspicion. No one, for example, would doubt the credentials of two Middlesbrough fans overheard in the following exchange after their team beat Everton in the FA Cup quarter-finals a few years back:

'So, the semis, eh?' says one. 'Aye,' his mate replies. 'More bloody expense.'

Over-exuberance among fans is seen as a hallmark of fakery, or even tastelessness. John Updike tapped into the latter viewpoint when he wrote: 'Few signs are more odious on the golf course than a sauntering, beered-up foursome obviously having a good time.'

In arguing that sport is primarily to be endured rather than enjoyed (as he does at length in the case of golf), Updike is perhaps showing his age. It's no coincidence either that the two Middlesbrough fans in the story above were, reportedly, 'elderly men'. Arguably, the older you get the more transient pleasure feels, and the more like trickery fortuitous sporting results seem. Personally speaking, sport gives me a momentary feeling of elation but increasingly that is followed by anticlimax and guilt. Once the dirty deed is done and I've watched a match on the box, I tend to feel more shame than pleasure. Brushing crisp crumbs from my crotch as I extract myself from the couch, my instinct, indeed, is to run straight to the Missus and ask whether it's too late to help with the family dinner.

I can't be alone in experiencing such emotions. Mind you, generalising would be a mistake. Driving home after watching France play Spain in the 2006 World Cup, newspaper columnist John Waters reported 'the distinct feeling of driving about 50 per cent above my usual standard, and [that he] knew it was down to Zinedine Zidane.' In his book *Fever Pitch*, Nick Hornby attributed occasional success with women to rare but pleasing Arsenal victories. These observations may not be as crazy as they sound, if a certain US study into the behaviour of sports fans can be believed. A psychologist at Georgia State University took saliva samples from soccer fans watching a match at the 1994 World Cup and found that testosterone levels rose markedly in those supporting the winning team. Some other psychological research suggests that sports fans suffer fewer bouts of depression and 'alienation' than do people who are uninterested in sports.

The case is far from proven, however. And there is a weight of evidence suggesting the reverse hypothesis, namely that spectators, as well as athletes, have higher-than-normal levels of stress, anxiety and hopelessness because of their engagement with competitive sport. Moreover, several studies have drawn a correlation between spikes in suicide rates in society and negative sports results. Frank Trovato, a sociology professor at the University of Alberta, published landmark research in the area in 1998, showing that Quebecois males aged fifteen to 34 were more likely to kill themselves when their local hockey team was eliminated from the early stages of the Stanley Cup. Trovato noted, in typical boffin-speak: 'The causal mechanisms for this effect are explicated in terms of a premature breakdown of the informal social context associated with the playoffs experience.' Other research suggests that sport provides fans with a temporary high but also a, perhaps fatal, temporary low. A sociologist at Central Missouri State University studied suicide rates in various US cities between 1971 and 1990, and concluded: 'Routinely reaching the playoffs could reduce suicides by about 20 each year in a metropolitan area the size of Boston or Atlanta.'

The problem here, of course, is that only a handful of

teams can reach the play-offs each year, and only one can win. The vast majority of fans who follow sport, thus put themselves at risk. Even if your team does well this year, it might flop the next, and how will you feel then? It's hard not to conclude that sport is, ultimately, a dangerous emotional crutch. Sport may paper over the cracks; it may keep us from asking too many dark questions; it may provide us with the odd moment of euphoria. But, in the end, Henry David Thoreau seemed to have hit the nail on the head when he wrote: 'A stereotyped but unconscious despair is concealed even under what are called the games and amusements of mankind.' Research shows that British men are far more unhappy in their 30s and 40s than at other times in their lives. Is it any coincidence that they spend much of these 'dark ages' watching football?

Again, personally speaking, the picture is somewhat fuzzy. I've a deep emotional connection to sport, which at times borders on the religious. At the end of each working week, my overriding thought is, 'What fixtures are on the box this weekend?' And, if the answer is 'bugger all', a mild depression sets in, mimicking the sort of gloom one feels during the Premier League off-season or in those desperately anticlimactic days after a World Cup Final.

Once my dependence on sport was altogether more profound. When I was in my late teens – and, typical for my age, moody and introspective – sport played a soothing, consoling and, at times it seemed, even life-saving role. My passion for horseracing, in particular, became an important part of my identity at a time when I was desperate to forge one (an identity, that is). I recall clearly days when I was depressed and downbeat and found relief by going to the racetrack. Travelling mostly with my racing-mad cousin Mick, but also sometimes alone, I would descend on far-flung meetings and do my absolutions. On returning home, I would feel – while not necessarily excited or invigorated – calmed and comforted, with an underlying sense that I was part of 'something'.

Daniel Wann PhD, an American psychologist who has studied the impact of sport on mental health, feels the sport-as-religion analogy is a valid one. 'People don't go to church as often as they used to. So one option – although not the only one – is sports fandom,' he says. 'By going to a game, or even watching it, you get that sense of tribalness, of community, of a common bond you can embrace.' If Wann is right in this regard, and sport is something of a surrogate faith in a Godless society, then perhaps we can learn something from research on the established links between religion and happiness (or unhappiness).

There are extensive studies in this field and they all point to the same thing: People with a strong religious conviction are happier than those without such a conviction. Psychologists are divided on whether people tend to be happy because they are religious, or religious because they are happy. But they all agree that a correlation is there, as evidenced by countless 'rate your happiness' surveys, as well as brain scan studies. One possible explanation for the link is the seemingly positive role of meditation on mental health. In an experiment that perhaps sheds some light on the issue, the psychologist Jon Kabat-Zinn once examined a group of office workers, getting half to meditate daily for eight weeks, and the other half to continue with their lives as normal. Four months after the experiment had ended, the people who had done the meditation were far happier than those who had not, as measured by EEG tests – scans which use electrodes to read positive feelings in the brain. Although meditation is more common to Buddhism than other religions, it can be found in non-Eastern faiths in such things as chanting and prayer. And perhaps it can be located in sport too – specifically in the trance-like state that is typically created by an afternoon alone listening to BBC Five Live.

Ultimately, however, we must be cautious about drawing rash conclusions. That is doubly so for 'people of faith', as those same people have, in different contexts, traditionally used their 'belief' as a default explanation for unexplained events.

As the physicist Richard P. Feynman pointed out, it's an all-too-human trait to wishfully think that higher forces are shaping our lives. The Nobel Prize-winner once opened a speech with the sarcastic anecdote: 'You know, the most amazing thing happened to me tonight. I saw a car with the licence plate ARW 357. Can you imagine? Of all the millions of licence plates in the state, what was the chance that I would see that particular one tonight?

Amazing!' Feynman's target was the unscientific soul who saw a cause-and-effect when there was none. The lesson should be learnt by every sports fan who likes to believe that his 'belief' makes him a happier person, a more successful person, a better driver, a better lover, or any number of other such things.

Perhaps the best that one can say for spectator sport in this field is that it helps to alleviate boredom, what Arthur Schopenhauer labelled as life's second-greatest burden (after survival). 'Life presents itself first and foremost as a task: the task of maintaining itself, *de gagner sa vie*. If this task is accomplished ... there then appears a second task: that of doing something with it so as to ward off boredom, which hovers over every secure life like a bird of prey,' wrote Schopenhauer. Some argue that boredom lies at the heart of human unhappiness in modern society. If so, then the diverting effect of sport may be making life literally more bearable. Let's be honest, though. It hardly feels like that when you're sitting through the average 90 minutes of soccer, in all its unremarkable glory.

Lie # 6: Sport is a win-win pursuit:

You can't have your cake and eat it. Sport is a constant drain on one's time and finances. The point is obvious enough, but it's worth underlining for the very reason that certain forces within the world of sport deny it to be the case. 'You *can* have it both ways' is the gist of Sky Sports' message. Or, in its own words, 'Join [us] ... to boost your entertainment and save you money. Subscriptions start at only £15 per month.'

Leave aside the paradox of saving money by spending money; what is most objectionable about this particular sales pitch is the absence of any reference to the real cost of a sports network subscription, namely the hours, days, weeks, months and years that you will never get back because you were watching Spanish league football or match play golf. The sin of omission is compounded by Sky when it claims that subscribers can enjoy '36,000 hours of sport each year'. That's over four years of sport – every twelve months. Even Motty would be hard pressed to watch all that.

Nike's mission statement, 'If you have a body you're an athlete', provides another glaring example of sporting double-speak. Not only is the statement plainly false, but it insults the intelligence of Nike customers. The implication is that if you're a couch potato who hasn't exercised properly in years, then you can become the next-best-thing to Ronaldinho or Paula Radcliffe – all for the price of a snazzy pair of trainers. In truth, being an athlete requires massive sacrifices. Youths entering professional sport must turn their backs on socialising with their peers. Relationships will have to be put on hold. Education may have to be suspended, and this can all take its toll on personal development. As Olympic swimming sensation Ian Thorpe once confessed, his chosen sport provided him with 'a safety blanket', insulating him from the outside world. Announcing his retirement from the discipline at the age of 24, he said he asked himself: 'What would my life be like without swimming? That was a very, very dark question.'

Being a serious sports fan also requires major sacrifices. Weekend DIY jobs have to go undone. Children's birthday parties have to be missed. And what of fandom's toll on personal development?

There are some people for whom sport is a healthy release. But for the average fan, sport is closer to being a wholesale escape from reality – an escape that can sap life of its very meaning. At least, that's the view of left-wing intellectual Noam Chomsky. In *Manufacturing Consent*, he claims that sport 'offers people something to pay attention to that's of no importance ... [and] keeps them from worrying about things that matter to their lives that they might have some idea of doing something about. And, in fact, it's striking to see the intelligence that's used by ordinary people in [discussions of] sports. I mean, you listen to radio stations where people call in – they have the most exotic information and understanding about all kind of arcane issues.'

Chomsky, of course, is making a political as well as personal point. He believes our obsession with sport has a retarding effect on society. He argues: '... to take apart the system of illusions and deception which functions to prevent understanding of contemporary reality, that's not a task that requires extraordinary skill or understanding. It requires the kind of normal skepticism and willingness to apply one's analytic skills that almost all people have, and that they can exercise. It just happens that they exercise them in analysis of what the New England Patriots ought to do next Sunday instead of questions that really matter for human life, their own included.'

Those familiar with Chomsky's work will not be surprised to hear that this dumbing down is allegedly orchestrated by right-wing business and political interests. By suggesting that the likes of the CIA want us to watch more sport, presumably so we pay less attention to their regime-changing activities, Chomsky may be overstating the case. But it's undeniable that media organisations – driven by their sponsors – do try to manipulate people's behaviour or consumption patterns and perhaps even their thought processes. Rupert Murdoch's Sky Sports, for example, would like you to believe that an early-season, Tuesday night fixture between QPR and Barnsley is a critical match of life-and-death which requires your undivided attention.

Chomsky is prescient, moreover, in highlighting the growing amount of collective energy and brainpower exhausted by spectator sports. Nerdish, statistic-loving obsessives were once figures of fun in the sporting world. But today they have a certain street cred. A recent fad is the creation of complex anagrams relating to pieces of sporting trivia – anagrams that are then circulated (for 'fun', you understand) on sporting websites, or published in fan-driven newspaper columns. In the midst of a major sporting controversy in 2006, for example, some sporto-linguistic obsessive worked out that the phrase 'the cricketing umpires Darrell Hair and Billy Doctrove' made up the following: 'Their verdict re cherry-colour ball: Pakistani meddling!' Is it just me who is a bit freaked out by this?

SPORT IS A DISTRACTION THAT THE WORLD TODAY CAN ILL-AFFORD

It's not that life should be joyless. Nor that we should be spending all our time watching the History Channel and reading worthy books on philosophy (although, if you're thinking of the latter, I can recommend my previous book …). It goes without saying that we – as humans – need to play. But surely we don't need to play to the detriment of our civilisation, or at the expense of our survival. What disturbs me is that I can explain to you in detail the 'active/non-active player' offside rule in football but I have only a vague notion about how global warming works. And I can hold forth on West Ham's league form, rattle off statistics on their goal-scoring and relay the latest team transfer gossip but I know next to nothing about a war that wiped out up to 4 million people in what is now the Democratic Republic of Congo between 1998 and 2003. Ask me about August 1998 and I can tell you that West Ham were then enjoying a rich vein of form in the Premership. I had to look up the fact that it was also the month the Congolese war started in earnest.

George Orwell once remarked: 'We have developed a sort of compunction which our grandparents did not have, an awareness of the enormous injustice and misery of the world, and a guilt-stricken feeling that one ought to be doing something about it, which makes a purely aesthetic attitude towards life impossible. No one, now, could devote himself to literature as single-mindedly as Joyce or Henry James.' Substitute 'sport' for 'literature' and 'Nick Hornby' for 'Joyce or Henry James' and you have a fair summation of the moral dilemma facing sports fans today. What with climate change, war in the Middle East and human rights abuses in Darfur and Burma, it seems to be irresponsible in the extreme to get worked up over West Ham's seasonal relegation dogfights.

If Chomsky is right, sport is the modern equivalent of Nero's Roman fiddle. We play it while the world burns.

In fact, sport may be worse than a distraction in that it gives people the illusion of being involved in important matters of state, whereas this couldn't be further from the truth. Italian philosopher Umberto Eco is strong on this point, condemning what he calls 'sports chatter' for the way in which it allows people fake engagement with politics. As a sports fan, you can conveniently adopt a phoney social conscience, he says.

Instead of judging the job done by the minister of finance (for which you have to know about economics, among other things), you discuss the job done by the coach; instead of criticizing the record of Parliament you criticize the record of athletes; instead of asking (a difficult and obscure question) if such-and-such a minister signed some shady agreements with such-and-such a foreign power, you ask if the final or decisive game will be decided by chance, by athletic prowess, or by diplomatic alchemy.

Whatever the truth of this, it's clear that sport's 'diverting' effect on the public has not been lost on politicians. Governments are known on occasion to release 'bad news' on big match days, believing – not without justification – that people glued to The Football or The Golf will not be interested in the latest hospital waiting list figures. Prime ministers and presidents have also used sport to manipulate public sentiment, and even to keep a lid on potential revolutions. Taking to heart George Macaulay Trevelyan's warning, 'If the French noblesse had been capable of playing cricket with their peasants, their chateaux would never have been burnt,' successive prime ministers have groomed themselves to appear as sporting 'men of the people'. Ted Heath made great mileage out of his passion for sailing, but soccer plays better with the gallery these days (for being less elitist) and thus Tony Blair could be found, during his term of office, on *Football Focus* offering his views on Newcastle FC's defensive formations. George W. Bush similarly helped to cultivate an 'Ordinary Joe' image by religiously watching *Monday Night Football* on ESPN (occasionally while eating/choking on pretzels). Elsewhere, politicians have used sport as a means of mobilising public support for their careers. From Italy to Mexico, owning a football team has been shown to be a major electoral asset. Hence, former Thai prime minister Thaksin Shinawatra's eagerness to take over Manchester City in the summer of 2007. The move coincided with a renewed campaign bid on his behalf to regain office in Thailand.

It should not be forgotten, moreover, that sport was deliberately used by some of the worst dictators of the 20th century, not only as a distracting device but as a vehicle for suppressing political dissent. Adolf Hitler once used an Olympics to rehabilitate his public image (as discussed in the next chapter). He also pioneered the use of state-run physical jerks to keep his country's mind on the war effort. Mussolini used soccer to strengthen his public appeal, claiming credit for Italy's 1938 World Cup victory. And Francisco Franco effectively stole football titles for Real Madrid to boost his public ratings. He went on to use that club's dominance to suppress regional – especially Basque and Catalan – identities.

The pattern continues today with North Korea's embracing of sport. Under the eye of Kim Jong-il, tens of thousands of Koreans participate in mass annual gym-nastics displays. Athletes who 'do their country proud' are lavishly rewarded, as illustrated in 2006 when North Korea won the under-20s women's soccer world cham-pionships. For 'defending the country and the spirit of waging dynamic ideological … battles', the team were awarded gifts such as 'deluxe cars and buses and flats'. Kim may well be attuned to the distracting effects of sport in another, more sinister sense. Was it just a coincidence that the dictator decided to stage two nuclear missile tests in the week leading up to the 2006 Fifa World Cup Final? (Incidentally, Israel also chose that week to launch its big-gest military offensive in years in the Gaza Strip.)

As we drift into the world of speculation, it's worth recording that two of the most celebrated literary depic-tions of a fascist or totalitarian society contain prominent references to either sport or its sister pursuit, gam-bling. In *Nineteen Eighty-four*, Orwell parodied what he saw as a modern obsession with state-sponsored play, commenting:

The Lottery, with its weekly pay-out of enor-mous prizes was the one public event to which the proles paid serious attention. It was probable that there were some millions of proles for whom the Lottery was the principal if not the only reason for remaining alive. It was their delight, their folly, their anodyne, their intellectual stimulant. Where the Lottery was concerned, even people who could barely read and write seemed capable of intricate calculations and staggering feats of memory.

Aldous Huxley had similar things to say in his signature novel, *Brave New World*, placing the delicious creation of 'Electro-magnetic Golf' at the centre of mankind's nightmarish future existence. This particular sport is played in the novel by higher-caste 'Alpha' members to the exclusion of the 'Betas', in a parallel of today's existing golfing apartheid. At one point, the novel's main protagonist, Bernard Marx, confesses that he believes the sport to be 'a waste of time'. To which his state-programmed companion replies 'in some astonishment': 'Then what's time for?' Eventually, Marx's seniors reprimand him for his 'heretical views on sport', and they banish him to an island for Alphas who have mentally lost the plot.

• The hallmark of a closed society is • an unhealthy obsession with sport

We haven't quite reached the stage where golf-haters are sent off to the loony bin but, arguably, we are getting close. Admitting that you don't possess a set of clubs is, in certain company, akin to confessing to being a communist; or worse perhaps, a teetotaller. In any event, you are not to be trusted. As for taking *no interest* in sport, there are few more subversive acts in society today.

In the past, religious and quasi-religious events – winter and summer solstice, papal visits, pilgrimages, Easter vigils and the like – were the definitive social unifiers, bringing old and young, men and women, and rich and poor together for a common purpose. Today, sport is our primary form of communion. Few people under 40 will be able to name traditional religious holidays outside of Christmas and Easter. But many would be able to rattle off at least approximate dates for important fixtures on the sporting calendar. No longer do we mark the seasons by the changing colours on a clergyman's robe, nor for that matter the movement of the sun, moon and stars. Rather, we know it's autumn because the Premier League is back in full swing. We know it's spring because Cheltenham is around the corner. And we know it's summer because it's wall-to-wall bleedin' Henmania, or – these days – Andymonium.

Actually, sport is now deliberately muscling in on religious holidays (which in fairness muscled in some time ago on pagan holidays – so let's not be too judgemental). When I was growing up, Sunday was still a relatively sports-free day. And, as far as I knew, if you played footie on Good Friday you would go straight to hell. Now, it's only Pope Benedict, Ian Paisley and a few other old-timers who raise a fuss about sport on the Sabbath. As for the feast day commemorating Jesus' crucifixion, it's the occasion these days of more than a couple of Premier League fixtures. It's surely only a matter of time before

Christmas Day is used as a relief date for games over the festive season.

TV viewing figures show how sport has moved into a league of its own, compared not only to religion but to political and military events. In Australia, for example, Roman Catholicism is listed as the largest religion in the country, with 5.1 million baptised followers. Yet the funeral of Pope John Paul II in 2005 could draw only 750,000 viewers – compared to 3.4 million viewers for the Aussie Rules Grand Final the same year. In the United States, the Superbowl attracted close to 100 million viewers in 2003 – 30 million more than the opening of Gulf War II. Such figures pale into insignificance, of course, compared to the 715 million viewers who tuned in to the Fifa World Cup Final on 9 July 2006, the most watched event in television history.

Inevitably, this trend is welcomed in certain quarters. According to Sepp Blatter of Fifa and IOC president Jacques Rogge, sport is spreading peace and unity by becoming something of a universal language, or global religion.

Such claims are examined in the next chapter.

CHAPTER 6

War Plus the Shooting:
Sport, Conflict and Prejudice

*'Sport is an instrument to help create a better world ...
If the world would accept the football rules we would not
have 70 conflicts in the world. We would have a more
peaceful world.'*
Adolf Ogi, United Nations special advisor on sport

'[Sport] will help save humankind'
Tatsuo Okado, head of Japan-based
Global Sports Alliance

*'As we proceed on our way towards 2010, the continent
(of Africa) and the African people will be better than they
are today thanks to the role of football.'*
Thabo Mbeki, President of South Africa, hosts of
the 2010 World Cup

There are myths about sport, and then myths within myths. One of the latter relates to George Orwell and his famous description of sport as 'war minus the shooting'.

The quote is trotted out by sports enthusiasts to suggest that Orwell agreed with the view that competitive game-playing is a sort of stepping-stone towards peace and reconciliation. But, as sociologist John Sugden points out, 'few sports optimists/evangelists quote the first half of Orwell's statement'. It runs so:

> Serious sport has nothing to do with fair play. It is bound up with hatred, jealousy, boastfulness, disregard of all rules and sadistic pleasure in witnessing violence.

'In other words: it is war minus the shooting,' Orwell continued, in an essay dating from December 1945. Dismissing the 'blah-blahing about the clean, healthy rivalry of the football field', he wrote: 'I am always amazed when I hear people saying that sport creates goodwill between the nations, and that if only the common peoples of the world could meet one another at football or cricket, they would have no inclination to meet on the battlefield. Even if one didn't know from concrete examples (the 1936 Olympic Games, for instance) that international sporting contests lead to orgies of hatred, one could deduce it from general principles.'

Not everyone will be convinced by Orwell's argument. Describing sport – as he does – as 'an unfailing cause of ill-will' is a particularly contentious claim because, theoretically, there is such a thing as friendly competition. But anyone who examines the issue in a detached fashion will see that Orwell was correct to reject the creed of sporting evangelists – the creed that says sport has special powers to generate brotherly love across the globe. Far from helping to end conflicts, sport has tended to trigger and prolong them. Sport has sometimes directly caused bloodshed, and frequently acted as a safe haven for forms of intolerance and hatred long-since dispatched from other realms of society. In fact, it could be argued that sport is a last refuge for racism, sexism, homophobia, animal cruelty, and perhaps bad language too, but we will come to that in a moment.

First, turn your mind back to when you were a child. Lined up in the playground, waiting to be picked for a team, this was your first truly competitive outing – your introduction to the world of sport. And what did it teach you? How to identify – and penalise – difference. If you were a bit overweight you'd be selected last and inevitably stuck in goal. If you were a girl, playing with boys, you would be deemed to be a handicap and told by your team-mates that *under no circumstances* should you touch the ball, or otherwise interfere with play.

A brutal philosophy of prejudice masquerading as realism is celebrated from our first serious kick of a ball. And throughout our sporting lives the philosophy is reinforced – ever more strongly the higher up the competitive ladder we climb. Men are segregated from women, able-bodied from disabled, black from white. Or so it has traditionally been in the sporting world. Some barriers have come down in recent times. But don't forget that, long after 'coloureds' fought alongside whites in European armies, they were prohibited from playing with whites in European tennis and golf clubs.

You may think it churlish of me to equate racial discrimination with differentiating on grounds of weight, or gender, in the school yard. The former, you might say, is sheer bigotry while the latter is about rewarding ability and punishing the lack of it. But, from a sporting perspective, all such forms of selection undermine the goal of universal participation – a goal purportedly pursued by sporting evangelists. The truth is that 'sport for all' is an oxymoron. Play can be for all but sport is – and has always been – an exercise in exclusion. It is inherently tied up with the identification of weaknesses, be they real or imaginary, 'natural' or inherited.

FAR FROM BEING A 'GREAT UNIFIER', SPORT HAS
• REINFORCED RACE, GENDER AND CLASS DIVISIONS, •
WHILE ALSO WIDENING THE GAP BETWEEN NATIONS

The problem with sports enthusiasts is that they see only the positive side. They describe sport as a bridge-builder, without acknowledging the barriers it has also erected. They talk about the Christmas truce of 1914, when rival troops at Flanders came out of their trenches and (allegedly) played a game of football with one another. But they never talk about the Soccer War – a dispute between Honduras and El Salvador which left 6,000 people dead. They give sport credit for its supposed role in keeping kids off the streets but they never take responsibility for its role in promoting violence and hooliganism.

Of all organisations, the International Olympic Committee (IOC) and the world footballing body Fifa are perhaps the worst offenders in this regard. The IOC breathlessly proclaims: 'Sport can help bridge cultural and ethnic divides, create jobs and businesses, promote tolerance and non-discrimination, reinforce social integration, and advocate healthy lifestyles.'

The IOC sees its own role as 'helping to build a peaceful and better world'. With similar modesty, Fifa claims to be 'making the world a better place through football'. Former European soccer bigwig Lennart Johansson is quoted on Fifa's website saying: 'The power of the Fifa World Cup TM is awe-inspiring. I can think of no other event in the modern era that can rival it for grandeur, beauty and emotion.' (Aw! It's so moving when you hear someone trade-marking their own words, isn't it?) Sepp Blatter has gone so far as to call Fifa 'one of the world's leading development agencies'. He has even had the temerity to compare himself to Nelson Mandela, once citing 'our [collective] work for the good of the world's young people, for example'. (Note the 'for example', as though Mandela and he had many other things in common.)

Sport's financial backers and business associates – the media included – sing a similar tune. According to sports giant Nike, 'the ability of sport, in particular football, to cross boundaries, inspire and to foster social cohesion is unparalleled'. But, significantly, sporting evangelism is not confined to those with a commercial interest in spreading the Good Word. The idea that sport is generally edging the world towards peace has been broadly accepted by pundits, politicians and the general public. Former United Nations Secretary-General Kofi Annan has spoken of sport's alleged ability to rise above politics and obtain goals with an ease that puts world governments to shame. 'The World Cup makes us in the UN green with envy,' Annan wrote in the summer of 2006. Not only had Fifa more members than the UN (207 compared to 191) but 'the World Cup is an event in which we actually see goals being reached,' including the goal of 'celebrating our common humanity', he said.

It's somewhat depressing that a UN Secretary-General would view a four-week piss-up in Germany as the pinnacle of international cooperation. Perhaps Annan had been taken in by those reports of Rwandese generals pausing during fighting in 1994 to watch the World Cup, then taking place in the United States. The story was seized upon by sporting evangelists as proof of sport's ability to stop wars. But the ceasefires in Rwanda, like those in the trenches of the First World World, were never more than temporary. And, in case one needed reminding, USA '94 did not stop the genocide that left 800,000 Rwandese dead. (Nor, incidentally, did the UN.)

Kofi Annan isn't the only politician to fall for the sales pitch of sporting evangelists. No one raised an eyebrow when he established in 2001 a new agency within the auspices of the UN with the grand title Office of Sport for Development and Peace, with the former president of Switzerland, Adolf Ogi, as its first director. Ogi promised to spread 'the sports message' across the globe, elaborating on his role in an interview with the BBC's Zeinab Bedawi in 2006.

Asked about corruption and drugs in sport, he told Bedawi to stop being so negative and think instead of the 'thousands, and thousands, and thousands, and thousands, and thousands' of people who played sport in developing countries and conflict zones. 'Sport is the last hope for them,' said Ogi, an ex-employee of the Swiss Skiing Federation.

'But,' asked Bedawi, 'are you really saying that sport can help India and Pakistan overcome their difficulties over the disputed territory of Kashmir?'

'Yes. Yes. Yes. It brings hope,' he replied.

'North and South Korea?'

'Yes,' replied Ogi. 'It brings hope to the small children who can play. They can forget they are in a difficult situation.'

THE POSITIVE IMPACT OF SPORT ON SOCIETY HAS GENERALLY BEEN OVERESTIMATED

Broadly speaking, the claims of sporting evangelists like Ogi fall under three categories. The first is that sport 'breaks down barriers' or otherwise erodes prejudice, the second is that sport promotes economic development, and the third is that sport helps to build nations or otherwise reduce violent conflict. Each of these claims can be examined with reference to commonly cited anecdotes – respectively Jesse Owens' triumph at the 1936 Olympic Games (a gathering of athletes already alluded to by Mr Orwell), the Republic of Ireland's qualification for Euro '88 (admittedly, a bit parochial, this one), and South Africa's victory in the 1995 Rugby World Cup.

1. Jesse Owens and sport's alleged role in 'breaking down barriers':

In the fantasy world of sporting optimists, the 1936 Olympic Games represented the triumph of good over evil. Under the very nose of Adolf Hilter, the African American sprinter and long jumper Jesse Owens claimed four gold medals – an impressive feat laden with political significance. A *Sunday Times* sporting anthology describes the episode as a 'black day for Hitler', while the IOC speaks of 1936 as 'the setting for great exploits' in which 'the athletes saved the honour of the Olympic Games'.

From such hype, you might be forgiven for thinking that Nazi Germany was defeated not on the beaches of Normandy but on the playing fields of Berlin. In truth, however, the 1936 Olympiad was an unadulterated success for Hitler and his henchmen. And, ironically, it was a success towards which Owens' on-field heroics contributed. Recall that Owens arrived in Berlin from a country that had been divided for decades along race lines. While at the Olympiad, he was allowed to travel with, and stay in the same hotels as, whites – something he was prohibited from doing in the US. Seeking to maximise American discomfort over the issue, German minister for propaganda Joseph Goebbels ordered the local media to show magnanimity towards African Americans, and refrain from insults or name-calling. Owens – for one – was impressed at the Germans' hospitality. Recalling that Hitler had even waved 'in my direction' from the stands, the track star said: 'I think the writers showed bad taste in criticising the man of the hour in Germany.' Others heaped lavish praise on the Nazis for their organisational nous. Not only was the Olympiad the first to be broadcast on television but it was the first to feature the Olympic Torch and other popular novelties, which helped to attract a massive 4 million ticket sales in Berlin. The *New York Times* captured the mood internationally, reporting that the games had put Germans 'back in the fold of nations', and even made them 'more human again'.

The IOC quite shamefully continues to deny the true impact of the 1936 Olympiad. Under the misleading heading 'no discrimination', the committee – in its official history of the games – states: 'During the 1933 [IOC] Session in Vienna, the Germans promised not to exclude German Jews from the national team.' What the IOC neglects to mention, however, is that Nazi Germany immediately reneged on this promise, banning all Jewish athletes from its squad, including at least one track champion. The Germans did allow one half-Jew to line out under the Nazi flag as a sop to the West. But, in the run-up to the games, it also sacked the respected builder of the Olympic village, Captain Wolfgang Furstner, from his post at the head of the German army's sporting programme – a move which prompted the Jew to take his own life.

Two prominent Jewish athletes on the US track squad boycotted the Olympiad in protest at Germany's blatant anti-Semitism but, shamefully, there was no show of solidarity from their political masters. Worse was a decision by the US Olympic track team to drop its remaining two Jewish athletes – suddenly and without proper explanation – on the eve of the 4×100 metre relay. One of the scratched pair later claimed that the decision was motivated by anti-Semitism and a desire on behalf of certain US Olympic Committee officials to save the Führer the embarrassing sight of two Yankee Jews on a winning podium. Whatever the truth of these claims, the episode certainly took the shine off Owens' fourth gold medal – for it was the African American who filled one of the two vacant places on what would prove to be a winning relay team.

All in all, then, it's hard to see Hitler doing anything else than rubbing his hands with glee at the end of the Berlin Games. Owens' triumph didn't rock Hitler's faith in Aryan supremacy and nor did it stop him from invading Poland three years later. The Olympics – with the connivance of the IOC – had made Nazi Germany look good. As well as scoring a huge propaganda victory, Hitler came away with the lesson reinforced that he could openly discriminate against Jews without a whimper of international protest. Historian Guy Walters believes the Games also gave Hitler confidence to accelerate his military campaign, starting in 1936 with the movement of 30,000 German troops into the Rhineland in breach of the post-First World War Locarno Treaty. 'Had the Games been boycotted, then Hitler would not have had the nerve to enter the demilitarised zone, because countries that boycotted sports were not countries that would have tolerated a breach of Locarno,' writes Walters. 'The world of sport had the opportunity to show the world of diplomacy the way, and it had let it slip.'

As for Owens, he continued to face discrimination in his homeland – something which casts doubt on the 'historic' influence of his feats on either side of the Atlantic. 'When I came back to my native country, after all the stories about Hitler, I couldn't ride in the front of the bus. I had to go to the back door,' Owens recalled. 'I couldn't live where I wanted. I wasn't invited to shake hands with Hitler, but I wasn't invited to the White House to shake hands with the President, either.'

Owens' feelings of deflation have been shared by countless other 'breakthrough' athletes. Boxer Francie Barrett carried the Irish flag at the opening ceremony of the 1996 Olympics in Atlanta but, on returning home, he still complained about being barred from pubs for being a Traveller. Hassiba Boulmerka defied death threats from Islamic extremists by competing in the 1992 Olympics in a conventional athletics outfit. But, on returning to her native Algeria (with a gold medal), she, along with other women in that country, were still 'subjected to discrimination in law and practice' – to quote Amnesty International.

So where is the evidence that sport breaks down barriers? Sport may well teach us something about foreign lands but knowledge comes with a price. Once we used to associate Iceland with fjords and the pop singer Björk. Now (if I am anything to go by) we associate it with former Chelsea striker Eidur Gudjohnsen and West Ham's ex-chairman Eggert Magnusson. Is that progress?

It would be nice to think that sport erodes prejudices. The problem is that prejudices are not easily eroded. Osama bin Laden went to see Arsenal play four times while he was staying in London in 1994. He bought merchandise from the club's souvenir shop for his sons. Perhaps he engaged in some friendly banter with fellow fans at the urinals. But, as journalist Simon Kuper notes, 'his affection for the game did not stop him from getting involved in a plot to massacre the American and English teams at the 1998 World Cup in France.'

A further point: Where prejudices are influenced by an episode in sport, they may not be influenced in a predictable way. It's not clear, for example, whether France's winning of the 1998 Fifa World Cup – with a team largely composed of 'immigrant' players – hardened or softened French attitudes to multiculturalism. To some, the victory was a lesson in how France would be stronger if all ethnic groups worked together. To others, including far-right politician Jean-Marie Le Pen, it was an illustration of how 'blue-blooded' natives were being marginalised in the France of today. In any event, there was no obvious improvement in race relations following the victory. Le Pen, who claimed that France 'would not recognise itself' in its footballing team, increased his electoral support after the World Cup, causing a major upset in the first round of the 2002 presidential poll. That serious ethnic strife remained in France was underlined by the inner-city riots of late 2005 involving French of North African origin.

The truth is that the emergence of a highly symbolic player like Zinedine Zidane can harden attitudes as easily as it can soften them. As Patrick Weil, a Paris-based political scientist, once commented: 'Our racists say, "If only all Arabs could be like Zidane".' Moreover, there are now two Zidanes: Zidane the national hero, and Zidane the national disgrace. When the French captain got himself sent off in the 2006 World Cup Final, Le Pen sympathisers rubbed their hands in glee. 'You can take the man out of the rough neighbourhood, but you can't take the rough neighbourhood out of the man,' said Thierry Henry after

Zidane's head-butting of an opponent. Henry was speaking in defence of his team-mate. But racists made a similar comment – with snide undertones – in condemnation of the 'African' Frenchman.

2. Euro '88 and the Celtic Tiger:

Little did Gary Mackay know that when he scored a winning goal three minutes from time in Scotland's final qualifying match for the 1988 European Championships, he would transform the fortunes of what was then Western Europe's poorest nation. Mackay's goal in Sofia meant that Bulgaria would fall short of qualifying for the championships in Germany – its place going instead to the Republic of Ireland.

An economic basket case, characterised by high taxes and outlandish corruption, the latter went into the tournament as a dead duck and emerged as a Celtic Tiger. Through a 1–0 victory over England at Stuttgart, and a narrow, exiting defeat to eventual champions the Netherlands, Ireland's image and understanding of itself was irrevocably changed. Thanks to Gary Mackay, Ray Houghton and Jack Charlton (only one of whom, ironically, had claims to be Irish), a nation of Thick Paddys and skinny peasants was transformed into a fat, rich, fecking financial miracle, characterised by low taxes and far more subtle forms of corruption. So the story goes, anyway – repeated ad nauseam by barstool economists across the land.

OK, OK, people don't always advance this thesis in total seriousness. But a toned-down version has gained common currency. The thinking runs that the success of the Boys in Green at Euro '88, and their further exploits at the 1990 World Cup in Italy, helped to boost confidence in Ireland domestically and overseas, thereby kick-starting the economy. But even this more modest theory has its problems. Why pick on soccer for a start? Johnny Logan won in the Eurovision Song Contest for Ireland in 1988. Why not credit him with boosting national confidence? As for directly linking football success with economic development, were it that simple, the average Brazilian should today be on the salary of someone from San Marino and vice versa.

Or, look at Cameroon: It qualified for Italia '90 on a wave of national euphoria, and went on to beat reigning champions Argentina before being eliminated by England in a game they dominated for long periods. What happened to Cameroon after the World Cup? The country's ranking on the UN Human Development Index fell to the point that in 2004 it was below its 1990 level.

It's not just barstool economists who attribute special wealth-generating powers to sport. Third World aid agencies are increasingly branching into the area, taking to heart Ogi's claim that 'development through sport is one of the most promising channels in human development today'. Once, such organisations used to limit themselves to handing out food and medicine. Now they also distribute such things as footballs and Uefa coaching badges. And they have been accompanied by a glut of new aid agencies purely devoted to sports-related projects. These include the French-based '*Sport Sans Frontières*', 'Right to Play' (the brainchild of former Olympic champion speed skater Johann Koss), and 'Football for Hope', Fifa's self-proclaimed Third World development wing.

While I have no wish to denigrate any such charity, you have to ask whether sports camps, for example, are any better at promoting development than music lessons or science expos. You also have to wonder just where the demand for sports-related projects is coming from. If you were living in a village without water, which would be more useful: a well in the ground, or a new home strip for the local soccer team? Fifa brags about its record of helping the Third World. But it mainly, if not exclusively, gives 'tied aid' – a now discredited form of development assistance. The world football authority sending money to Africa for it to build stadiums is about as commendable as the EU sending money to Africa for it to buy Belgian chocolates.

A final myth in the area of sports and development deserves attention, namely the myth that hosting a major sports tournament is great for the economy. Even a self-proclaimed sportophobe like Ken Livingstone has been taken in by the belief that staging an Olympic Games is a licence to print money. When the London mayor was first approached about the 2012 bid he was less than enthusiastic about the idea. His then antipathy towards sport had extended in large part from unpleasant memories of his PE teachers at school, whom he once likened to 'rehabilitated Nazi war criminals'. This aside, whatever doubts he had about sport's intrinsic value quickly receded once the 2012 marketing men got to work on him. Having started out as an Olympic sceptic, Livingstone quickly became one of the greatest advocates of the London Games. But what are the advantages of staging an Olympics, and do they outweigh the disadvantages?

Most recent Olympiads have cost the host country vast sums of money – and the London Games look set to be no different. Staging a single-sport 'World Cup' or world championships may be a little less risky as there is a greater chance of finding gainful employment for stadiums after the event. However, there is no guarantee of an economic boon – as the hosts of the 2007 Cricket World Cup discovered. In the immediate aftermath of the event, economists predicted a fall-off in tourism to the Caribbean because of negative publicity over perceived organisational chaos, and the controversial death of cricket coach Bob Woolmer. *The Economist* magazine once summed up the situation thus: 'The economic arguments for hosting big sporting tournaments are largely spurious ... Tourism gets a boost but only temporarily. Evidence from Sydney and Barcelona, hosts of successful recent Olympic Games (and tourist spots long before that), suggest long-term tangible gains were negligible.'

3. South Africa and the Rugby World Cup:

One of the most heart-warming images of modern sport was surely Nelson Mandela's appearance at the final of the 1995 Rugby World Cup, holding the trophy aloft with the winning Springboks captain, François Pienaar. For most of the previous three decades, Mandela had been confined behind bars, while the South African rugby team was perhaps the most potent symbol of the hated apartheid regime that had put him there.

The preserve of whites for so many years, the Springboks had belatedly moved to fielding mixed teams. One coloured player made the line-up for the 1995 final. It was not so much this development, however, as Mandela's gesture that defined the World Cup, an event described by Africa historian Martin Meredith as 'a moment of national fusion'. He recalls: 'When the Springboks went on to win the match, in one of the most intense afternoons of physical endeavor and emotion that any of those present were ever likely to witness, the whole of South Africa erupted in celebration, blacks as joyful as whites.'

The occasion was undoubtedly a memorable one. But what did it actually achieve? Meredith describes the event as 'the climax to Mandela's [reconciliation] efforts'. But, at the same time, it didn't stop about 1 million whites – a fifth of the white population – from leaving South Africa in the first decade of democracy. Some of these exiles can be seen each year unfurling the Vierkleur flag of the old apartheid government at Test matches at Twickenham and elsewhere. As for those whites who remained, let's be honest, did they look into their hearts and respond to Mandela with a reciprocal gesture? 'By and large, the white community does not seem to have shown an appreciation for the incredible magnanimity of those who were the major victims of a system from which they [the whites] benefited so much,' Archbishop Emeritus Desmond Tutu remarked in 2006.

Professor Albert Grundlingh, a South African historian based at the University of Stellenbosch, is one of a number of academics who believe that the impact of his country's first World Cup victory has been overstated. Speaking ahead of the 2007 Rugby World Cup Final, he said: 'The sense of unity [in 1995] was not real but it was deemed to be real.' He added that the occasion was 'in many respects an orchestrated media affair'.

But let's assume the 1995 World Cup did bring blacks and whites closer together. Who should take the credit? Certainly not the sport of rugby in South Africa. One of the first things the local rugby establishment did after the tournament was to sack its reformist chief executive Edward Griffiths – a man who had insisted that all the players sing *Nkosi Sikelel' iAfrika*, the new national anthem, before each match. 'If there is to be a relationship between rugby and the black majority, the World Cup has done no more than cause their eyes to meet,' Griffiths said. 'There will have to be a long courtship before there can be any thought of marriage.'

Today there is not so much a marriage between rugby and the black majority as a sordid, exploitative affair. The leading clubs, which remain almost entirely in white hands, have resisted change at every turn. The South African rugby union, SA Rugby, has been forced to introduce informal quotas but even these are being implemented in a mean-spirited fashion. As one South African news magazine commented, 'For some coaches SA Rugby's commitment to development means putting two blacks on the wing where they won't get too much of the ball.' The result could be seen in 2007 when South Africa won the Rugby World Cup for a second time with a team composed of thirteen whites, two players of mixed race – or 'coloured' ethnicity – and no blacks. It represented little transformation in twelve years.

Naturally, if you listened to sporting evangelists you'd think it was the game of rugby that defeated apartheid, secured South Africa's transition to democracy and gave birth to the Rainbow Nation. But if sport had such powers then why are they not replicated elsewhere? In Nigeria, there was widespread euphoria surrounding the country's national soccer team in the 1990s. As well as winning an Olympic Gold Medal in 1996, the Super Eagles qualified for their first-ever World Cups in 1994 and 1998, drawing plaudits across the globe. But there was no shift towards national unity in a country wracked by tribalism. One historian notes that towards the end of the 1990s 'so many violent disputes broke out … – over land, politics, religion, ethnicity, money – that at times it seemed that Nigeria was ungovernable.' When Iraq won the Asian Cup in Jakarta in July 2007, Baghdad was momentarily awash with jubilant football fans. But 24 hours later the city was back to grim normality, with the murder of more than 60 people in two bombings. In fact, the civilian death toll *rose* in August 2007 to 1,770, an increase of 7 per cent on the previous month.

That is not to say that sport is incapable of having a positive influence on conflict situations. The Northern Ireland human rights activist Don Mullan has written about how sport inadvertently kept him away from violence during the height of the Troubles in the early 1970s. An avid goalkeeper for his local youth club in Derry, Mullan grew up with a love of football and specifically of Gordon Banks, the England stopper who was credited with 'the greatest save of all time' against Pelé in a World Cup match in 1970. Mullan was an eyewitness to Bloody Sunday, the killing of fourteen people by British soldiers in Derry in 1972. After the event, some of his peers joined the IRA and Mullan said he had been tempted to follow. There were both family and other personal reasons that helped to keep him away from violence. 'But, without a doubt, my hero-worship of Banks was an important factor too,' Mullan wrote in *Gordon Banks: A Hero Who Could Fly*. 'My respect for a man who had such a positive impact on my life helped contain my rage. I just knew that *Banksy* was a good man and, with the simplicity of an adolescent's thinking, I knew too that there had to be fair-minded and decent British people like him.'

Such experiences cannot be discounted. But they shouldn't lead us to believe that all cases of hero-worshipping promote the cause of peace. One of the pin-up boys of Croatia's separatist movement was Zvonimir Boban, a footballer with Dinamo Zagreb who famously karate-kicked a Yugoslav policeman during riots surrounding a soccer match between his home club and Red Star Belgrade in 1990. Boban, who went on to play with AC Milan in Italy and to captain Croatia's first independent side, was a particular favourite of Dinamo fans who, it's no coincidence, were strongly represented in the Croatian army. In fact, football played an especially prominent role in the former Yugoslavia as a recruitment force for nationalists. Arkan, the Serbian war criminal, was head of the Red Star fan club. It was through that organisation that he helped to train countless angry young Serbs in methods of street violence and terror.

Today the Dinamo–Red Star riots, which took place at the Maksimir stadium in Zagreb on the eve of Yugoslavia's disintegration, are remembered by a statue of heroic soldiers under the west stand. The inscription reads: 'To all Dinamo fans for whom the war started on 13 May 1990 and ended by them laying their lives on the altar of the Croatian homeland.'

Today also you can find fresh instances of football sucking young men into violent insurrection. From

London to Krakow, right-wing organisations flock to football, seeing it as rich territory for recruitment. This continues a long tradition stretching back at least to 1932 when the British Union of Fascists (BUF) adopted sports fanaticism as a cornerstone of its identity. Praising 'the sprit of British manhood' as embodied in its games, BUF leader Oswald Mosley once remarked: 'The only methods we shall employ will be English ones. We shall rely on the good old fist.'

Think to yourself: Would the world be better off without sport? You may answer that the question is immaterial. The fact is, you might say, we are stuck with sport (just as we are stuck with religion), and so all we can do is to try to create a form of sport (and religion for that matter) that does more good than harm.

It's certainly the case that attempts to weigh up the pros and cons of sport from a societal perspective are hugely inconclusive. If you look at the role of football on conflict situations, for example, it appears on a surface level to have started more wars than it finished. Look below the surface, however, and the picture becomes less clear. The famous Soccer War had as much to do with poverty and long-simmering political tensions in Latin America as it had to do with the contentious scoreline, 'El Salvador 3, Honduras 0'. In fact, Ryszard Kapuscinski, the Polish journalist who brought the conflict to the world's attention, said the 'real reasons' for the war were over-population, competition between Honduran and Salvadoran peasants over access to land, and allied migration problems. Kapuscinski wrote: 'Newspapers on both sides waged a campaign of hate, slander and abuse, calling each other Nazis, dwarfs, drunkards, sadists, spiders, aggressors and thieves. There were pogroms. Shops were burned. In these circumstances the match between Honduras and El Salvador had taken place.'

The most comprehensive examination of sport's role in conflict was conducted by the journalist and author Simon Kuper in his award-winning study, *Football Against the Enemy*. Kuper travelled to various parts of the globe, investigating the precise role of soccer in generally miscreant political affairs. No definite conclusions were reached, but it's noticeable that, twelve years after initially publishing the work, Kuper launched a new edition with the not-too-cheery sub-heading: 'How the world's most popular sport starts and fuels revolutions and keeps dictators in power' (no mention of 'stopping revolutions or putting democrats in power').

In an article in the *Financial Times* in 2005, Kuper wrote, in a somewhat more considered tone: 'Every now and then sport does marginal good or harm, but most of the time it makes no difference whatsoever.' And perhaps this is the fairest conclusion one can reach on the matter. Sport unleashes passions but these can work for good or evil in a political context. Euro '96 saw a resurgence in nationalist pride in the tournament's host-nation England. But it also saw a Russian student being stabbed in the neck purportedly for 'sounding German' – after England lost to the Old Enemy in the semi-finals.

A few years ago, American journalist Franklin Foer repeated Kuper's odyssey across the footballing globe, focusing specifically on the game's 'globalised' nature. And, significantly, he joined Kuper in reaching a downbeat conclusion. 'Wandering among lunatic fans, gangster owners, and crazed Bulgarian strikers, I kept noticing the ways that globalization had failed to diminish the game's local cultures, local blood feuds, and even local corruption,' wrote Foer. 'In fact, I began to suspect that globalization had actually increased the power of these local entities – and not always in such a good way.'

An overriding question in all of this is: What, if anything, does sport stand for? Is there some kind of political – or pseudo-religious – ideal inherent to sport that we would like to see, or not see, spread around the world? The rhetoric of Blatter and Co. implies that sport operates on a moral plane 'above politics'. And many fans accept this as a given. Indeed, a common refrain within sporting fraternities is that politics is a grubby and cynical business, whereas sport is pure and idealistic. Some fans seem to disparage politicians in direct proportion to their worshipping of sports stars. But are they right to do so?

Nelson Mandela once said: 'Sport can reach out to people in a way which politicians can't.' On reflection, this is far from being a compliment. Yes, sport is a potentially useful vehicle for spreading, say, anti-racism messages but this is only because sport is a hotbed of racism. It is *because* sport is home to so many uncivilised traits – xenophobia, knee-jerk machismo, rabid nationalism, and so on – that it is useful politically. The 1995 Rugby World Cup is illuminating in this context. Whatever good that came from the event was *despite* sport – and particularly despite South African rugby and all it stood for – rather than because of it. The reason why Mandela's pitch-invasion was such a powerful gesture of peace was the very fact that he was walking into an arena of deep-seated prejudice.

Far from being 'above politics', sport is more accurately described as 'below it'. Certainly, the history of sport is riddled with examples of political leaders forcing sporting ones to face up to their moral responsibilities.

• Sporting organisations don't transcend politics; they ignore it out of expediency •

South Africa is a case in point. Long after most of the world's governments had moved to ostracise the apartheid regime, rugby unions in the British Isles and elsewhere continued to send touring parties to the pariah state. In 1977, Commonwealth governments signed the Gleneagles Agreement, calling for an end to all sporting contacts with South Africa. But this was largely ignored by key figures in sport. In as late as 1985, the All Blacks tried to put together a tour to the apartheid state and were stopped by the New Zealand High Court. The following year, a team composed mainly of All Black players travelled to the country anyway.

Before rushing to eulogise the world of sport, Kofi Annan should have read this particular chapter of history. For it's clear that, on the whole, politicians took the lead in tackling South Africa over its racist policies while sportspeople – administrators, athletes and fans – generally lagged behind.

More precisely, *certain* politicians took the lead against apartheid (notably the Labour Party in the UK) while other politicians (notably the Conservatives under Margaret Thatcher) hardly blazed a trail. The point remains, however, that politicians – as a collective – tried to effect change, while sportspeople – almost en masse – attempted to maintain the status quo. A telling exchange came early in the anti-apartheid struggle when Denis Howell, Minister for Sport under James Callaghan's Labour government, met Albert Agar of the Rugby Football Union to urge the four 'home unions' to boycott South Africa. 'We saw the Minister out of courtesy,' said Agar after the 1974 meeting. 'I don't envisage any further contact.'

Significantly, it wasn't just sporting 'blazers' who stuck their heads in the sand over the issue. Sports fans, in general, told politicians to stop interfering with their 'sacred' games. Writing about his experiences as an anti-apartheid activist in the UK, Peter Hain recalled that some of the worst beatings meted out to 'Stop the Tour' campaigners were from England rugby fans rather than from the police.

As for the IOC, to its credit, it banned South Africa from the Olympic Games as early as 1964. In truth, however, this was less a reflection on the moral fibre of the Committee than on the realpolitik of the situation. Were the IOC to have allowed South Africa to compete, it would have faced a major protest from its African affiliates. Tellingly, the IOC barred that other racialist state Rhodesia from the Olympics only after African governments had threatened to withdraw their teams from the 1972 Munich Games. The IOC's then president Avery Brundage showed his true colours by likening the barring of Rhodesia from the Olympiad to the massacre of Israeli athletes by terrorists at the same event. The 'two savage attacks', as he called them, were equivalent in his mind, for both impinged on the IOC's autonomy.

Of course, the IOC has a habit of being on the wrong side of history (which gives you little hope for Beijing 2008). Despite all of the corruption scandals recently linked to the organisation, it has expelled just one official in its 113-year history: Ernest Lee Jahnke, an American delegate who encouraged athletes to boycott the 1936 Nazi Games.

In 1968, the IOC – backed by its US affiliates – convicted American track stars Tommie Smith and John Carlos of 'grossly unethical conduct', and sent them home early from the Mexico Games. The duo's crime was to give a 'black power salute' on the podium when collecting their 200-metre gold and bronze medals. Not only were the two Americans ostracised by the Olympic movement and vilified by the sporting press, but so too was Peter Norman, the Australian 200-metre silver-medallist, who expressed sympathy for the US pair. Norman was dropped by the Australian Olympic team for the 1972 games, despite performing well in trials. His later life was characterised by depression and alcohol abuse, and he died of a heart attack in October 2006.

Other sporting organisations are equally fastidious about keeping 'politics' out of their realm. The International Cricket Council threatened to fine Australia more than £1 million for boycotting a planned tour to Zimbabwe in 2007. Uefa *did* fine Robbie Fowler – a total of 2,000 Swiss francs in 1997 – for lifting his football jersey to reveal a T-shirt expressing support for sacked Liverpool dockers. A penalty such as this is purportedly aimed at protecting the integrity of sport. But, in practice, it reveals a dishonesty at the heart of Uefa and like-minded sporting organisations. For a start, governing bodies are all too happy to nose into political affairs if their interests are at stake.

When the FA, for example, wants money to build a new stadium, it comes knocking on the door of politicians. But when politicians seek financial accountability, or question decision-making within football, they are told by the FA to stay out of 'internal matters'. Fifa are past masters at this particular game, threatening countries with expulsion from international competitions in the case of 'political interference'.

In 2000, the world footballing body told Brazil it would be barred from the World Cup if its government went ahead with an investigation of alleged corruption in the Brazilian Football Association. In 2006, Fifa similarly told the Trinidadian government to back off in its investigation of a ticket sales controversy. 'No government in the world can intervene in Fifa's business ... and that's the bottom line,' Fifa's vice-president Jack Warner said at the time. In 2007, Fifa was at it again, trying to block a Polish government investigation of alleged match-fixing. After threatening to ban all Polish teams from international football competitions, Fifa successfully got a number of officials who were suspended from the Polish Football Association reinstated in their positions.

Why, in any event, would sport want to stay out of politics? (Why specifically would the IOC want to do so, unless it meant it could avoid awkward questions about, for example, its decision to give the 2008 Games to China?) Furthermore, were it desirable to stay out of politics, it's clearly not possible. As Aristotle said, everything is political. Or, as sports journalist Tom Humphries put it (a little more pertinently): 'Politics and sport always mix. In grants, in swimming inquiries, in civic receptions, in anthems, on days of sheer flagwaving nationalism. They mix. Always.' Sporting organisations can't have it both ways. They can't claim to be both making the world a better place and staying out of politics. 'Making the world a better place' is a political act.

• SPORT WILL DO BUSINESS WITH ANYONE •

You might be willing to cut sporting organisations some slack if you felt they were motivated by anything other than greed. But look at who sport does business with? Probably the three industries with which it has closest ties (after gambling) are drinking, smoking and prostitution.

• SPORT IS A MAN'S WORLD (AND THAT MAN IS NEANDERTHAL MAN) •

It was treated as a light-hearted story. 'SCORING IN THE SOCCER LOVE SHACK' 'PROSTITUTES WORK OVERTIME FOR THE CUP.' Colourful descriptions circulated in the press of fans arriving in Germany with jaw-dropping giddiness at the services on offer. In Cologne, an establishment claiming to be Europe's biggest brothel draped an 80-foot poster of a semi-naked woman on one of its side walls. The slogan read: 'A Time to Make Friends.'

But how many women were trafficked to meet the demand? In advance of the tournament, one campaign group claimed that as many as 40,000 illegal immigrants, mainly from Eastern Europe, would be smuggled into Germany for the World Cup sex trade. This appeared to have been a considerable over-estimation. But even if the figure was 400, or 40, the football establishment should surely have been concerned. Instead, it overwhelmingly rebuffed calls from a range of organisations – including Amnesty International – for it to back measures aimed at combating 'forced prostitution'.

And what do we now discover? South Africa, the next hosts of the Fifa World Cup, are considering legalising prostitution (along with public drunkenness) for the duration of the tournament in 2010. There may well be merits to decriminalising prostitution in a well-managed environment that offers health screening, education and other supports for women in the sex trade. But what is being mooted in South Africa, a country incidentally with a shockingly high rate of HIV infection, coupled with a chronic problem regarding the physical and sexual abuse of women, is simply to lift an already flimsy sex trade ban for no other purpose than to satisfy the demands of a visiting army of randy Europeans.

We will have to wait and see how Fifa deals with such issues in 2010. All we can say for now is that the organisation has a track-record of insensitivity to feminist concerns. A few years ago, Blatter called on women soccer-players to line out in 'tighter shorts' in a bid to boost their TV ratings. Adopting his usual God-like tone, he announced: 'Let the women play in more feminine clothes like they do in volleyball.' (To which England national goalkeeper Pauline Cope replied: 'typical of a bloke.') Former Uefa president Lennart Johansson once expressed a view similar to Blatter's, saying: 'Companies could make use of a sweaty, lovely looking girl playing on the ground.'

But it's not just administrators who exhibit chauvinism in sport. Athletes can be just as bad. You couldn't imagine a Dutch politician describing a group of his lady peers as 'lazy, fat pigs' but a Dutch tennis player did so without flinching. Admittedly, Richard Krajicek subsequently clarified his controversial contention that female players shouldn't be allowed on the show-courts at Wimbledon. 'I said 80 per cent of the top 100 [women] are fat pigs but I just over-exaggerated a little bit. What I meant was only 75 per cent,' he remarked.

Yes, women athletes do make more money today than in the past but only, it seems, by better dancing to the tune of men. The earning power of the US women's soccer team leapt considerably after it won the 1999 World Cup Final. The result was a factor, but not as significant as defender Brandi Chastain's decision to whip off her top to reveal a sports bra after scoring the winning penalty.

Off the pitch, women adorn sport like cherries on a trifle. Clear your mind and think of a woman's place in sport and you'll see a dolly bird in a bikini, walking around a boxing ring with a placard in her arms; or a grinning blonde holding an umbrella over a racing-car in a pitlane; or a near-naked teenager dancing on the sidelines of an American football game; or a couple of pouting ladies standing behind a trophy presentation at some race meeting; or a bevy of beauties in the swimwear edition of *Sports Illustrated*. Oh, the many sporting uses to which a woman can be put! In the mid-90s, West Ham United decided to jazz up its half-time entertainment. So out went the traditional, unadorned run-out and target practice by the substitutes bench, and in came The Hammerettes, a barely legal troupe of erotic dancers who stirred the crowd with high-kicks and flashes of their pompoms. And this from a club that purported to uphold old-fashioned, 'family' values. (Thankfully, the Hammerettes were 'transfer listed' by the club's Icelandic owners at the start of the 2006/07 season. The girls were reportedly quickly snapped up by London neighbours Leyton Orient for a career in new colours.)

Leaving women aside, let's look at the other two products with which sport is so closely allied: cigarettes and alcohol. It's fair to say that since sports sponsorship began, the games' governing bodies have had addictions to both. First, they couldn't survive without the advertising revenue of tobacco firms, and now they cling to the drinks industry like strung-out junkies to their dealer. The Carling Cup. The Heineken Cup. The Guinness Premiership. The John Smith's Grand National. So many major events flavoured with the taste of alcohol.

Given their supposed role in promoting healthy lifestyles, sporting bodies are sometimes criticised for doing business with the spirits industry, or – as the case may be – the cigarette trade. Their defence is similar to that of rogue nations who have been caught supplying weapons to despots. 'If we didn't take the business someone else would,' says every organisation from the FA to the Oxford and Cambridge university boat clubs – the latter of which had, until recently, Beefeater Gin as the sponsor of their annual boat race (confirming what we know already: there is no concrete difference between amateur and professional ideals).

Some defenders of drinks sponsorship blather on about how sport will suffer without its money. But defenders of tobacco sponsorship made the same claims – until their bluff was called. Neil Macfarlane, Margaret Thatcher's one-time sports minister, expressed what was once a commonly held view when he wrote the following doom-laden words, with their somewhat jingoistic subtext: 'It is no use saying that other companies will emerge and take the place of the tobacco industry. What we will then get are Japanese and American high-technology companies taking television time for audiences outside the United Kingdom. What will happen to events like the Benson and Hedges golf and snooker and cricket? The John Player cricket league and the Embassy world matchplay snooker? What about motor racing? These and many other sponsored events bring enjoyment to millions and, just as important, jobs to thousands.'

It's something of a disgrace that certain sports, including motor racing, are still campaigning – and campaigning successfully – to have cigarette companies advertise with them. Where is the moral leadership? For much of the past 40 years, sport has tried to circumvent legislation aimed at restricting cigarette advertising. And, if current trends are anything to go by, it will spend the next 40 years resisting outside interference with its drinks sponsorship deals. Heineken illustrated how companies try to push the boat out during the 2007 Rugby World Cup. A lobby group campaigning against alcohol addiction was forced to go to court during the tournament to get the Dutch brewer to comply with France's controls on the advertising of alcoholic drinks. The court ordered Heineken to remove certain adverts, giving it 48 hours to take action or face fines.

The relationship between sport and alcohol runs deeper than sponsorship, however. 'Win, lose, on the booze', is the motto of the average sports fan. Or, as Homer Simpson once put it to Bart, 'Son, when you participate in sporting events, it's not whether you win or lose, it's how drunk you get.' To some people, watching a match without downing half-a-dozen pints is as unnatural as Mass without the Eucharist. Again, the odd tipple isn't at issue. The problem is when drinking gets out of control, as it frequently does around sporting fixtures.

Every so often, the state has tried to interfere with the sports fan's God-given right to get sloshed on match day, and it has been soundly rebuffed. In the late 19th century, for example, a court in Ireland imposed a ban on alcohol at race meetings in Cork because of an outbreak of public drunkenness. The sporting press reportedly went 'apoplectic' over the ruling, which was inevitably rescinded. An editorial in a sporting newspaper at the time screamed: 'Is it not a monstrous interference with the liberty of a subject to withhold from the respectable and temperate classes a glass of wine or a bottle of beer [so] needed on a racecourse during a long day?'

Attitudes in sport have changed little since then, and even the football stadium disasters of the 1980s, and the hooliganism which accompanied them, failed to generate a more 'sober' approach. After the Heysel disaster, in which 39 people were killed, a drinks ban at stadiums was introduced, but within weeks it was scrapped when clubs complained of lost revenue.

Deep down, there appears to be a dependency problem, or an addiction to alcohol that runs through every level of sport. For my part, I can't imagine being a sports fan and *not* drinking. Every major sporting occasion in my life was tied up with booze – from Guinness-soaked competition tours with my college rowing club, to day-long benders watching World Cup fixtures in my local pub.

SPORT IS A REFUGE FOR RACISM, HOMOPHOBIA
• AND SIMILAR UNCIVILISED TRAITS – NOT A RELEASE •
FROM THEM

Sport isn't just home to a drinking culture. It's also home – albeit to a lesser degree – to racist and homophobic ones. The late Bernard Manning made a healthy living as an after-dinner raconteur at football clubs the length and breadth of Great Britain. The 'comedian', who said 'I'm no racist, I take the piss out of puffs too,' is probably the closest thing the football terraces have to a patron saint.

'Does your boyfriend know you're here?' is the chant that most commonly greets travelling Brighton fans, their city being famed for its large gay population. 'He shoots, he scores, he eats your Labradors – Ji-sung Park,' is one a series of tributes sung about Manchester United's South Korean midfielder. A related chant goes (to the tune of 'Lord of the Dance'): 'Park, Park, wherever you may be, You eat dogs in your home country, But it could be worse, you could be a Scouse, Eating rats in your council house.'

And these are considered the funny ones.

'I'd rather be a Paki than a Jew' was sung by West Ham fans when Spurs visited Upton Park in March 2007 – which just goes to show how little has changed. When I attended the same fixture some years previously I heard virtually identical racist slurs. Not only were there derogatory comments about the Tottenham supporters' supposed 'Jewishness', but one of the visiting team's Eastern European players was greeted with the menacing ditty: 'Where's your passport?'

In fairness, there is less overt racism in soccer than before. The monkey chants and bananas flung at former England midfielder John Barnes by sections of his own support seem like a very distant memory. Yet there is still a sense among football fans that they can get away with saying things in a stadium that they could not say on the streets outside. The question here is not whether racism in sport has gone down (it clearly has) but whether it still outstrips racism in other walks of life.

For one example of how sport lags behind politics specifically, look at Glasgow's Old Firm rivalry. Unionists and nationalists from Northern Ireland can today hold cordial meetings at the Stormont Assembly. But Celtic and Rangers fans can't sit in the same stadium together without breaking into choruses of 'Ooh, ah, up the 'ra [IRA]' and 'We are the billy boys … up to our knees in Fenian blood'.

On homophobia, there is a more clear-cut case against sport. At the start of the 2007/08 Premier League season, the FA introduced new rules banning anti-gay hate-speak – about four months after such speech had been made illegal under UK Sexual Orientation Regulations, and exactly 40 years after the decriminalisation of homosexuality. While the FA's move was welcome, it served only to remind us how much catching up football – and sport in general – needed to do in the area. When tennis legend Billie Jean King was outed as a lesbian by her ex-girlfriend in 1981 she lost all her endorsements within 24 hours. Martina Navratilova estimates that she lost about $12 million in sponsorship deals when she was pushed out of the closet in the 1980s. Today, it appears to be easier to 'come out' as a cabinet minister than as an athlete. As footballer David James once asked: 'If one in ten people are gay, where are all the gay Premiership stars?' In the history of English football, only one professional player has revealed himself to be gay. Eight years after doing so, Justin Fashanu took his own life.

• SPORT IS HOME TO SOME MIXED-UP ATTITUDES •
TOWARDS ANIMALS

A final topic deserves mention in this chapter, if only because those to whom it relates can't speak for themselves. The issue is animal welfare.

Sport has a history of abusing and torturing defenceless creatures: from gamecocks – incorporated in the original Sport of Kings – to dogs, rats, bulls, bears, hares, foxes and today, to a large degree, horses. Yes, yes, thoroughbreds *are* generally well-treated in horseracing. Some receive five-star boarding and a pleasant retirement at the stud farm once their racing days are numbered. But how many others leave the track either for the local knacker's yard, or a much worse fate – export for slaughter in harsh conditions, following possible abuse or neglect at the hands of new owners?

No one knows exactly. And, until recently, no one cared. No one that is except Carrie Humble, a feisty Formby-born horsewoman who in 1993 set up the Thoroughbred Rehabilitation Centre in Lancashire. The initiative was two-pronged: first, to show how ex-racehorses could be retrained for other, useful purposes; and second, to draw attention to issues of animal welfare which the sport had overlooked. One of her first customers was Hallo Dandy, the 1984 Aintree Grand National winner, who was discovered in a field almost exactly a decade after his most famous victory, in a dishevelled and emaciated state. A steady stream of custom followed – too much for Humble to deal with alone. Today she has up to 30 horses in training at any one time at her yard. But the British Horseracing Authority (BHA) estimates that at least 300 horses leave racing each year with no obvious home to go to, and campaigners put the figure at closer to 3,000.

Responding to negative criticism over the issue, the BHA set up a fund in 2000 to support Humble's charity and two other like-minded groups. The Retraining of Racehorses fund had a budget of £360,000 in 2007 – this for a sport with annual prize-money of £100 million, and with an off-course betting market of over £10 billion. While Humble welcomes the industry's investment, she admits it is a 'tiny drop of water on an enormously big boulder'.

Humble's efforts have been duplicated in other countries – but not without difficulty. In the affluent South African province of Western Cape, a group of owners agreed some years ago to fund a local thoroughbred rehabilitation centre to the tune of £25,000 a month. The funding was withdrawn in April 2007, however, when the charity, the South African Society for the Prevention of Cruelty to Animals (SPCA), passed a resolution at its AGM expressing its opposition to horseracing on welfare grounds. The funding was later reinstated – but only after the SPCA assured the owners it was not actively campaigning against the sport.

Humble, who won an MBE in 2003 for her campaigning efforts, admits attitudes are changing in horseracing but 'there is a long, long, long way to go'. She says: 'There are people who are concerned about the reputation of the sport. The racehorse is more protected than it has ever been but don't think humanity has changed. There are still atrocious trainers, atrocious breeders, and atrocious owners.'

Horseracing's responsibility to retired racecourse performers is but one issue that cries out for attention. We balk at cases like 'marathon tot' Budhia Singh, who in 2005 ran a 60-kilometre race across India at the age of three. But racehorse trainers may be guilty of putting their charges through a similar ordeal by rushing them to the gallops as yearlings, when their bodies are underdeveloped. 'I would still have deep concerns about racing young animals,' says Humble. 'I don't want to sound like a tree-hugger, or a cuddly-bunny, but these horses go through a lot.'

And what about putting thoroughbreds around the giant fences of Aintree? Do horses really enjoy the Grand National, as we are so frequently told by their handlers? Do horses really need to whipped during racing? What responsibility, if any, have punters towards those 'bets' of theirs who break their necks, or otherwise suffer fatal injuries, on the course?

As with all sports, horseracing is avoiding asking such awkward questions of itself. Presumably, it fears the relevant answers might spoil the fun.

A postscript to this discussion comes from Bernard E. Rollin, a philosophy lecturer at Colorado State University with a particular interest in animal rights issues. Some years ago, he held a meeting with members of the college's Rodeo Club to discuss ethical aspects of their favourite sport. The philosopher initially received a cool response but, after a while, he got the two-dozen-odd cowboys at the meeting to start asking questions about whether the sport was inherently cruel, whether certain practices – like roping calves – should be banned, and how to tally the way in which they treated animals in rodeo with their self-proclaimed respect for animals on the ranch.

Rollin said he sent the youths out of the room to discuss the matters without his interference. He recalled:

Fifteen minutes later they came back. All took seats in the front, not the back. One man, the president of the club, stood nervously in front of the room, hat in hand. 'Well,' I said, not knowing what to expect, nor what the change in attitude betokened, 'What did you guys agree is wrong with rodeo?' The president looked at me and quietly spoke: 'Everything, Doc.' 'Beg your pardon?' I said. 'Everything,' he repeated. 'When we started to think about it, we realised that what we do violates our own ethic about animals.'

The next part of Rollin's story is illuminating.

'Okay,' I said, 'I've done my job. I can go.' 'Please don't go,' he said. 'We want to think this through. Rodeo means a lot to us. Will you help us think through how we can hold on to rodeo and yet not violate our ethic?'

As Rollin tells the story, we don't know whether the cowboys left that meeting and became advocates for the rights of cattle, or whether they returned to their conventional rodeo ways. But their initial response to Rollin's questioning is revealing – for it reminds us how sometimes in life we reach a juncture where we know that something we are doing is wrong but we don't want to act upon that knowledge. We stall (like Rollin's cowboys when they asked for his further assistance). We try to reconcile wrong with right, and stick with wrong until the square is circled. We long to have our cake and eat it – to have it both ways.

Conclusion

In May 2007, Sepp Blatter was re-elected for a third term as president of world footballing body Fifa. Ensconced in the post for a further four years, he will by 2011 have held office for longer than many a Pope has lasted in the Vatican, or many a dictator has withstood the march of democracy. Fittingly, his reappointment was announced to the world through a somewhat Orwellian communiqué.

'Those of the 207 Fifa member associations present who were eligible to vote have returned Fifa President Joseph S. Blatter for a third term of office until 2011 with a standing ovation. A boy then handed him a globe as a symbol of Fifa's new slogan "For the Game. For the World", the self-proclaimed 'supreme body' of global soccer declared, in a statement that brought to mind images of a vaguely Stalinist elevation.

A patriarchal figure for not just soccer but world sport today, 'Uncle Joe' presides over an expansionist church. If the latest Fifa figures can be believed, football now has more followers than either Christianity or Islam. (One in five people were said to have watched some of the 2006 Fifa World Cup).

The religious analogy is apt – for soccer in particular, and sport in general, has muscled in on parts of life which were traditionally the preserve of churches. Not only that, but sport has embraced some of the unhealthiest aspects of religion: fanaticism, judgementalism and irrationality, to name but a few.

If I have occasionally, in this book, been overly harsh on sport, it's only because there is a distinct lack of self-criticism within the church of Cardinal Blatter. Sport today appears to occupy a special place in society – above censure. In the Western world especially, you can satirise religion, you can poke fun at Jesus, you can write like Richard Dawkins does. But dare to label sports fans as delusional and you'll be met with a wall of intolerance bordering on hatred.

Of course, you do get commentary within sport that masquerades as self-criticism. Sports fans will rabbit on about the supposedly pernicious influence of professionalism and the commercialisation of sport, while possibly slouched in an armchair dressed in a £50 replica football top, sipping the 'official' beer of their favourite team, and channel-hopping between Premier League fixtures on the TV.

Fans like to blame everyone but themselves for what's wrong with sport. Worse, they create scapegoats, and seek lazy explanations for the way in which things have turned out. Professionalism is not all bad, and the commercialisation of sport is, well, wholly predictable when all fans seem to want is more live matches on the box.

The reality is that the sins of sport run deeper than Rupert Murdoch and the shrill tones of satellite television football coverage. They run deeper than egotistical multi-millionaire club owners, than Ben Johnson and latter-day dopers, than big money and big-time hype. Yes, all of these phenomena may be manifestations of a sporting world gone wrong. But none can exclusively take the blame.

I venture that sport starts to go wrong as soon as it's taken too seriously. And that can happen in a school playground as easily as it can happen in an Olympic stadium. It can happen in the mind of an athlete who values winning above all else, or in the heart of a spectator who becomes a manic obsessive.

Sport has the potential to educate, to bring joy, to enrich lives and to promote understanding between different peoples. But it won't get there if it's left in the hands of the game's hierarchy. Anyone who cares about sport, and believes that it's more than just the foul play it has become, has a contribution to make.

I mean 'foul play' here in a very specific sense – as tarnished, or corrupted, play. Such play is far removed from the innocent play of children. It has become detached from the creative play of artists – musical, literary, athletic, or otherwise. And it stands firmly opposed to the questioning, Socratic play of life's dabblers, not to mention the sort of play Einstein had in mind when he said 'play is the highest form of research'.

Perhaps what is needed in sport is something akin to a reformation – a bottom-up reclaiming of the pursuit by those who genuinely value it most. For a fan, that might mean flexing your consumer muscles, and also reappraising whether, in fact, you want to be fanatic. For an athlete, that might mean training on your own (ethical) terms, and also questioning the actual meaning of success.

It's perhaps a little fanciful, but one could argue that sport – as today's dominant religion-of-sorts – is at a juncture in its history similar to that faced by Christianity close to 500 years ago. Under the papacy of Leo X, the Catholic Church had become a cynical exercise in wealth generation. The then Pope sold his followers 'indulgences' – tickets to salvation – to fund pet projects (all for the glory of God, you understand). Today, Sepp Blatter flogs executive boxes and prawn cocktail buffets for a dream no less lofty than St Peter's Basilica: A world united for 90 minutes, possibly with extra time and penalties, under the banner of a trademarked soccer tournament.

With Christianity, reformation came in 1517 when a German theologian called Martin Luther decided to have it out with Pope Leo. The Augustinian monk went to a chapel in Saxony and nailed to the front door a treatise that critiqued the Catholic Church. Unforeseen by Luther, the gesture marked the start of the Protestant Reformation, a historic schism in organised Christianity.

With sport, the time may be ripe for similar action, and in that spirit I am nailing this treatise to the door of

Fifa's headquarters in Zurich, or at least posting it through the letterbox with a polite covering letter. Naturally, I'll invite Fifa to respond to my assertions, and you can go to www.joehumphreys.com to see what reply, if any, I get.)

The world of sport needs to be challenged, and if that leads to a split between two realms of worship, then so be it. Let Blatter lead one crusade! We, right-thinking sports fans can lead another. (Are you with me? Let's be 'aving you!)

What sort of sporting world could we create? Well, I for one, have a dream. With apologies to Martin Luther (King, this time) … It's a dream rooted in the ideals to which I have been exposed as a Catholic-educated, some-what guilt-ridden, white, Anglocentric, middle-class male who has spent an inordinate amount of his life watching and playing sports.

I have a dream that one day I can watch football with a clear conscience, that there is enough justice in the world to allow me waste an afternoon in front of the box.

I have a dream that one day sport will capture the best aspects of play. On that day, sport will return to its rightful place at the end of the news – after the weather and *News for the Deaf*. Athletes will blush if they win and shrug if they lose, and anyone who uses the word 'tragedy' in relation to a sporting contest will be roundly laughed out of it.

I have a dream that one day football analysts will find useful employment in society. I dream of fewer sporting events on TV, and of important fixtures that one has to actually attend in person in order to witness. I dream of untelevised World Cups – if only for the novelty value.

I have a dream that one day sport will be genuinely tolerant, and be played truly without barriers; that one day Africa will win the Ryder Cup. I have a dream that sports fans will take the Special Olympics as seriously as they take the Olympic Games, and I dream that neither is taken too seriously.

I dream that one day the three-legged race will become an IOC-approved discipline. And, on that day, how great it would be if an Israeli–Palestinian combination won gold! I have a dream that the sporting authorities will admit that they can't prevent athletes from cheating – so let's stop getting so sanctimonious about the whole thing. I dream that the record books will stop listing who won, and instead tell the stories of those who took part.

I have a dream of Olympiads without expensive opening ceremonies, and of Superbowls without war-mongering half-time shows. I dream that one day, due to public demand, Sky opens a pay-per-view philosophy channel. I dream that one day it will be possible to openly dislike sport and still secure high public office.

I have a dream that one day people will rise from their couches and shed their replica football jerseys as though they were school blazers on graduation day. I dream that they will then switch off their television sets, and decide – on reflection – against getting drunk on a Sunday afternoon. I dream that they will collectively proclaim, with heartfelt determination: 'Actually, the final scores from Wentworth can wait.' And when it happens, we can join hands – men and women, religious believers and secularists, Arsenal supporters and regular people – and sing in unison: Free at last! Free at last! Thank God Almighty, we are free at last!

NOTES

INTRODUCTION

'Absolutely devastated …': RTE Radio 1, *Liveline*, 18 November 2005.

'Academics researching … [Best]': *The Economist*, 3 December 2005.

'I saluted my people … [Di Canio]': *The Irish Times*, 14 December 2005.

'[Mussolini] basically a very principled …': Paolo Di Canio, *The Autobiography* (London: CollinsWillow, 2001).

'In 2005, a World Cup qualifying game …': Viewership figures from AGB Nielsen Media Research, 2005.

'BBC's coverage of Mexico vs. Iran … [vs. *Songs of Praise*]': *Guardian*, 'World Cup Holds Up Well in the Heat', 12 June 2006; http://www.bbc.co.uk/religion/programmes/songsofpraise/features/did_you_know/.

'2.5 million average weekly audience for *Songs of Praise* …': http://www.bbc.co.uk/religion/programmes/songsofpraise/features/did_you_know/.

'What is soccer …': Sean Wilsey, 'Why the World Loves Soccer', *National Geographic*, June 2006.

'To a very large extent [truth] …': John Kenneth Galbraith, *The Affluent Society* (Boston: Houghton Mifflin, 1958).

'The unexamined sporting life … [Bannister]': Foreword to Peter McIntosh, *Fair Play: Ethics in Sport and Education* (London: Heinemann, 1979), p. v.

CHAPTER 1: SPORT AND STUPIDITY

'From a 25-man squad … [Meyer]': *The Irish Times*, 15 November 2004; *Daily Telegraph*, 11 November 2004.

'Comparative IQ tests ...': As cited in Jeff Merron, 'Taking Your Wonderlics', espn.com, http://espn.go.com/page2/s/closer/020228.html

'Riding on the edge ... [Lott]': Darren Lott, *Street Luge Survival Guide* (Gravity Publishing, 1998).

'Old football captain ...': As cited in Paul Rouse, 'Sport and Ireland in 1881', in Alan Bairner ed., *Sport and the Irish* (Dublin: UCD Press, 2005), p. 13.

'Cheerleading ... [injury rate]': Bill Pennington, 'Pompoms, Pyramids and Peril', *New York Times*, 30 March 2007.

'They make you sign a medical release ...': Ibid.

'A study in New Zealand ... [gymnastics]': R.N. Marshall and H. Sandes, 'Dunedin Sports Injuries 1974–76', as cited in McIntosh, *Fair Play*, p. 186.

'Dr Derren Ready ... [gym bugs]': As cited in Peta Bee, 'Is Going to the Gym Bad for Your Health?', *Daily Mail*, 4 July 2006.

'We are not in trouble ... [Fox]': As cited in Vicky Frost, 'Gym Shirkers Unite!', *Guardian*, 5 October 2006.

'Sports injuries comprise one-third of all injuries ...': D.G. Uitenbroek, 'Sports, Exercise, and Other Causes of Injuries: Results of a Population Survey', *Research Quarterly for Exercise and Sport*, 67, 380–85, 1996.

'[Soccer] ... cost the British taxpayer about £1 billion': N. Rahnama, T. Reilly and A. Lees, 'Injury Risk Associated with Playing Actions During Competitive Soccer', *British Journal of Sports Medicine*, 36, 354–9, 2002.

'750,000 report to casualty ...': K. Hoey, 'UK is Still Way Behind When it Comes to Sports Medicine', *Daily Telegraph*, 18 November 2002.

'We need to ask ourselves whether it is better for a child to break a wrist ...': 'Bumps and Bruises Are "Good for Children"', *The Times*, 12 June 2007.

'In the US, some educators are questioning ... [obesity]': See, for example, Angela Lumpkin, Sharon Kay Stoll and Jennifer Beller, *Sport Ethics: Applications for Fair Play* (St Louis: Mosby, 1994), pp. 50–60.

'A recent survey of athletes … [blacks in US colleges]': National
     Collegiate Athletics Association survey, as cited in Earl
     Ofari Hutchinson, 'Sports Still No Ticket Out of the Ghetto',
     AlterNet, 2 January 2003.

'Educational cripples …': Ibid.

'I regret bringing her into this sport … [Dongmei]': As cited in
     Ching-Ching Ni, 'Former Athletes Speak of Beatings and False
     Promises', *Los Angeles Times*, 13 May 2007.

'My fifth grade teacher would be surprised to see me now …
     [Ronaldo]': *Hello!*, 988, September 2007, p. 131.

'[Mori] … surveyed 105 captains of industry': Catriona Davies,
     'Captains of Industry Tend to be Good Sports', *Daily
     Telegraph*, 5 January 2005.

'If fine bodies … [survey]': Nelson Mandela, *Long Walk to
     Freedom* (London: Abacus, 1994), p. 233.

'[rugby] concussions …': *Pretoria News*, 17 August 2007.

'There have been calls in the US for compulsory headgear …
     [soccer concussions research]': Sean Gregory, 'Head Games',
     Time, 29 November 2007.

'jogging solo …': *Daily Mail*, 22 March 2006.

'Soccer heading injuries …': See research by Dr Adrienne Witol
     at the Medical College of Virginia in Richmond, as cited in
     'Study Links Injuries to Head Impacts in Soccer', *New York
     Times*, 14 August 1995. Also, see discussion in Aidan P. Moran,
     Sport and Exercise Psychology: A Critical Introduction (Hove:
     Routledge, 2004), pp. 255–6.

'Beijing soccer spectator …': Reuters, 29 June 2006.

'Brazil … [reading survey]': *The Economist*, 18 March 2007.

'I was ostracised … [McInally]': George Kimball, 'America at
     Large', *Irish Times*, 2 March 2006.

'In 1990, when England played Cameroon … [Hornby]': Nick
     Hornby 'Faded Glory: Taming the Hooligans', *National
     Geographic*, June 2006.

'lunacy … [football] the great retardant': Nick Hornby, *The
     Omnibus (Fever Pitch)* (London: Indigo, 1992), pp. 59, 114,
     188.

'I rarely *think* …[Hornby]': Ibid, p. 8.

'kinesthetic sense …': David Foster Wallace, 'The Beauty of Roger
    Federer', *Guardian*, 7 September 2006.
'Had the tensions between the real Zidane …': Simon Barnes,
    'How Zidane's Belief Brought Him Down', *The Times*, 16 July
    2006.
'I wanted men conceited enough …': Jimmy Hill, *Independent*,
    3 July 2007.
'Side-spin … [balls]': Craig C.M. et al., 'Judging Where a
    Ball Will Go: the Case of Curved Free Kicks in Football',
    Naturwissenschaften, 2006. pp. 93, 97–101.
'Concluding that …': Russell Gough, 'Moral Development
    Research in Sports and Objectivity', in M.J. McNamee and
    S.J. Parry eds., *Ethics and Sport*, (London: Taylor and Francis,
    1998), p. 146.

CHAPTER 2: SPORT, CHARACTER AND MORALS

'Obviously, it's hard to fulfil Christian ideals …': *The Irish Times*,
    16 November 2005.
'give his body constant exercise … [Rousseau]': From *Emile*
    (1762), as cited in McIntosh, *Fair Play*, p. 24.
'marauding the countryside …': Ibid, p. 27.
'Fighting with fists is the natural and English way …': Thomas
    Hughes, *Tom Brown's Schooldays*, 1857, Part 3, Chapter 5.
'[rugby] antidote to the poison of effeminacy …': Nick J.
    Watson, Stuart Weir and Stephen Friend, 'The Development
    of Muscular Christianity in Victorian Britain and Beyond',
    Journal of Religion and Society, Volume 7, 2005, para 2.
'the two unmentionables of the Victorian period …': Ibid,
    para 21.
'football … would be the means to teach the world's masses …
    [Rimet]': John Lichfield, 'World Cup Founder Hoped to Use
    Sport to Unite Humanity', *Independent*, 11 June 2006.
'*Play Up Kings!*': As quoted in D.J. Taylor, *On the Corinthian Spirit*
    (London: Yellow Jersey Press, 2006), p. 85.

'Play the game … [*NY Times*]': As quoted in James W. Keating, 'Sportsmanship as a Moral Category', in Jan Boxill ed., *Sports Ethics: An Anthology* (Blackwell, Oxford, 2003), p. 66.

'A strong body of qualitative and quantitative research exists …': Lumpkin, Stoll and Beller, *Sport Ethics: Applications for Fair Play*, p. 189.

'lower level moral reasoning …': Brenda Jo Bredemeier and David L. Sheilds, 'Moral Growth Among Athletes and Nonathletes: A Comparative Analysis', *The Journal of Genetic Psychology*, 147(1), 7–18, 1986.

'Egocentrism is the hallmark …': Bredemeier and Sheilds, 'Game Reasoning and Interactional Morality', *The Journal of Genetic Psychology*, 147(2), 257–75, 1986.

'It's a fairly mythical idea … [Moran]': Interview with author, 30 August 2007.

'[tchoukball] striving after prestige …' International Tchoukball Federation, http://www.tchoukball.org/. See also: Tchoukball Association of Great Britain, http://www.tagb.org.uk.

'I never actually severed all my safety nets … [O'Toole]': *The Irish Times*, 27 July 1996.

'[football] a vehicle for love …': David Winner, *Those Feet: An Intimate History of English Football* (London: Bloomsbury, 2005), p. 2.

'the big and terrifying statement …' Julie Myerson, *Not a Games Person* (London: Yellow Jersey Press, 2005), p. 2.

'something magical happens … [Moran]': Interview with author, 30 August 2007.

'They [fathers] are happy to wax lyrical …': Sarah Harris, *Daily Mail*, 22 March 2006.

'I had to put back my marriage … [O Cinneide]': *The Irish Times*, 21 January 2006.

'Jomo Sono …': Eric Miyeni, *O'Mandingo! The Only Black at a Dinner Party* (Johannesburg, Jacana, 2006), p. 125.

'Priorities have changed in footballers … [Keane]': *Guardian*, 15 August 2007.

'[Klinsmann] unforgivable …': *Daily Telegraph*, 16 March 2006.

'(parents) humiliating children …': TNS Social Research, 'Good Sports – On and Off the Field', Australian Sports Commission, August 2005.

'Kingsley vs. Newman': Watson, Weir and Friend, 'The Development of Muscular Christianity in Victorian Britain and Beyond', para. 17.

'[sport] a training ground for elitist bullies …': John Sugden, 'Sport and Community Relations in Northern Ireland and Israel', in Bairner ed., *Sport and the Irish*, p. 241.

'Virtue consisted in winning …': George Orwell, 'Such, Such Were the Joys', 1952.

'the spirit of the Anglo-Saxon … [Pickford]': As cited in Winner, *Those Feet*, p. 243.

'Rugby is cleaner … [Robbie]': Interview with author, November 2006.

'rugby cannon fodder …': McIntosh, *Fair Play*, p. 104.

'behaviour verging on psychopathic …': Ibid, p. 102.

'[professionalism] end of the *Chatterley* ban …': Taylor, *On the Corinthian Spirit*, p. 107.

'[Olympics] contributing to the professionalisation of sport …': McIntosh, *Fair Play*, p. 138.

'sport ethic … [over-conformity]': Jay Coakley, 'Ethics, Deviance and Sports: A Critical Look at Crucial Issues', in Alan Tomlinson and Scott Fleming eds., *Ethics, Sport and Leisure: Crises and Critiques*, Chelsea School Research Centre Edition, Vol. 1 (Aachen, Germany: Meyer and Meyer Verlag, 1995), pp. 13–20.

'Dalai Lama … [volleyball]': As quoted in Simon Eassom, 'Games, Rules and Contracts', in McNamee and Parry, *Ethics and Sport*, pp. 71–2.

'Besides its obvious beneficial effects … [Buddhist view]': 'Sport and Society', *Soka Gakkai International Quarterly*, 45, July 2006.

'Sport, *when practised in the right way* …': Pope Benedict XVI, *L'Osservatore Romano*, 21 September 2005.

'In addition to a sport that helps people ...': Pope John Paul II, 'During the Jubilee of Sports People', *L'Osservatore Romano* (English edn.), No. 46, p. 9, 15 November 2000.

'[sport] that protects the weak ...': Kevin Lixey, 'Why the Church "Believes" in Sport', The 2nd Magglingen Conference on Sport and Development, Switzerland, December 2005.

'*Muskeljudentum* ... [Nordau]': As quoted in Franklin Foer, *How Football Explains the World* (London: Arrow, 2005), p. 67.

'synagogue and school ...': 'A History of Jews in Sport', *Encyclopedia Judaica*, http://www.jewishsports.com/jewsin/history/oldhistory.htm.

'the battlefields of *jihad* ...': Y. Al-Qaradawi, *The Lawful and the Prohibited in Islam* (Indiana: American Trust Publications, 1994), p. 293.

'[gambling on] elephant race ...': M.I. Al-Kayasi, *Morals and Manners in Islam* (Leicester, England: The Islamic Foundation, 1986), p. 191.

'[utilitarianism, dichotomy] ... playing to win': Sigmund Loland, 'Fair Play: Historical Anachronism or Topical Ideal?' in McNamee and Parry, *Ethics and Sport*, pp .95–8.

'Never ridicule or yell at your child ...': Australian Sports Commission, Codes of Behaviour, 2002.

'[Council of Europe] fair play ...': Recommendation No. R (92) 14 Rev, of the Committee of Ministers to Member States on the Revised Code of Sports Ethics, 1992.

'egg and spoon race ... [sports day]': http://news.bbc.co.uk/sport1/hi/funny_old_game/3041339.stm, BBC, 19 May 2003.

'Chinese gymnastics ... [Pinsent]': BBC, 17 November 2005.

'Coaches should first try to create a positive moral environment ...': Thierry Long, Nathalie Pantaleon, Gerard Bruant and Fabienne d'Arripe-Longueville, 'A Qualitative Study of Moral Reasoning of Young Elite Athletes', in *The Sport Psychologist*, Human Kinetics, 2006, pp. 330–347.

'No one does that kind of work ... [Moran]': Interview with the author, 2007.

Chapter 3: Sport, Cheating and Judgementalism

'Johnson probably wouldn't know what a steroid is … [Pound]':
As cited in Daniel Benjamin, 'Shame of the Games', *Time*,
24 June 2001.

'Most people loved the entertainment … [Johnson]': *The Times*,
24 September 2003.

'That run, the electrifying run …': Simon Barnes, *The Meaning of
Sport* (London: Short Books, 2006), pp. 120–1.

'[Johnson] … in a state of shock': *Time*, 24 June 2001.

'Chris Evert … [overruling umpire]': As cited in McIntosh, *Fair
Play*, p. 78.

'I've not had a go … [Redknapp]': Guy Hodgson, 'Di Canio: Saint
or Sinner?', *Independent*, 18 December 2000.

'When Paolo did his act of sportsmanship …': BBC Online,
http://news.bbc.co.uk/sport1/low/sports_talk/1073945.stm,
16 December 2000.

'Ulama, an Aztec ball game …': For a discussion on the game, see
The Economist, 24 April 2004.

'What goes on in the middle … [Kitchen]': As quoted by Rodney
Hartman, 'Umpires Hit for Six in the Face of Poor Decisions',
Pretoria News, 4 April 2006.

'Casey Martin … [and disabled bowler]': Anita Silvers and David
Wasserman, 'Convention and Competence: Disability Rights
in Sports and Education', in William J. Morgan, Klaus V. Meier
and Angela J. Schneider eds., *Ethics in Sport* (Champaign, IL:
Human Kinetics, 2001), pp. 417–18.

'Oscar Pistorius … [and IAAF attitude]': Associated Press, 'IAAF
Proposes Rule Which Would Keep South African Amputee
Sprinter Out of Beijing Games', 31 May 2007; 'Blade Runner
Furious at IAAF', *Sunday Telegraph*, 15 July 2007.

'[Nostalgic games] … are played with whoever shows up':
feminist Janice Moulton, as quoted in Morgan, Meier and
Schneider eds., *Ethics in Sport*, p. 415.

'anti-social behviour orders … [and crime rates]': *The Economist*,
3 February 2005.

'[Ronaldo] ... dart board': *Sun*, 'Give Ron One in the Eye', 3 July 2006.

'Eamon Dunphy ... [on Ronaldo]': *The Irish Times*, 11 December 2006; *Daily Mail*, 17 April 2007.

'Graham Poll ... [abuse]': Scott Murray, Guardian Unlimited, http://football.guardian.co.uk/worldcup2006/minbymin/0,,1788392,00.html, 22 June 2006; hate-site, http://www.121s.com/viewtopic.php?t=9243&postdays=0&postorder=asc&start=18; and *Sun*, 23 June 2006.

'[Poll] said such abuse was a key factor ...': *Inside Sport*, BBC, 4 June 2007.

'[Fandel] ... inexcusable mistake': *Sunday Telegraph*, 29 May 2007.

'Steve McClaren ... [fans' abuse]': *Sun*, 29 March 2007; *The Scotsman*, 30 March 2007; *Independent on Sunday*, 30 March 2007.

'No British newspapers ... [1953 England vs. Hungary]': Winner, *Those Feet*, p. 127.

'like a feral beast ... [Blair on the media]': *Guardian*, 13 June 2007.

'One of the more nauseating ...': Michael Steinberger, *Financial Times*, 10 August 2002.

'Toilets were smashed ... [Neville celebration]': *Independent*, 28 January 2006.

'Buachallan Buidhe ... [Deasy]': As quoted in Fintan O'Toole, 'Record We Cannot Be Proud Of', *The Irish Times*, 17 January 2005.

'We should be saying we are not going to win ... [Komphela]': *Sunday Times*, Johannesburg, 15 July 2007.

'In life, you have to move on ... [Keane]': *The Irish Times*, 4 November 2006.

'Kiwi eye-gouging ... [Sinkinson's defence]': *New Zealand Herald*, 16 April 2006.

'Let's not get distracted ...': David James, 'Don't be Tough on the Refs', *Guardian*, 9 February 2007.

'South African football bosses ... [marijuana ban]': *Pretoria News*, 'Aren't They a Bunch of Dopes?', 7 December 2006.

'Frankie Sheahan ban … [sentence reduced]': *The Irish Times*,
2 September 2003.

'[Keane] … still be banged up': Rod Liddle, *The Sunday Times*,
20 November 2005.

'athletes' fundamental right …': Wada Anti-Doping Code, 1 June
2007.

'potentially massive placebo effect … [Keen]': As quoted in
'Elite Sports Coaching in Practice: Ethical Reflections – an
Interview with Peter Keen', in Tomlinson and Fleming eds.,
Ethics, Sport and Leisure: Crises and Critiques, pp. 44–5.

'studies have since shown that athletes taking placebo drugs
…': 'How to Cheat Without Cheating', *The Economist*,
3 November 2007.

'drug-free crusader … [Millar]': 'Millar Changes Gear to Sign for
Anti-doping Team', *Guardian*, 31 July 2007.

'[Wada rules] … rabidly fascist': Neville Cox in an interview with
the author, August 2007.

'Doping is organized … [Pound]': *Los Angeles Times*, 7 July 2007.

'Sports bodies never enter into discussion … [Cox]': Interview
with the author, August 2007.

'Young athletes who take heavy doses … [Tennant]': *Time*, 24
June 2001.

'the best fisherman …': John Gray, *Straw Dogs* (London: Granta
Books, 2002), p. 196.

'If an athlete risks her health …': As cited in Andy Miah,
'Genetically Modified Athletes', *Ethics in Sport* (London:
Routledge, 2004), p. 158.

'one million American children … [growth hormones]': Lincoln
Allison, 'Sport Should Accept Inevitable and Legalise Use of
Drugs', *The Irish Times*, 12 August 2004.

'I'm not a cheat … [Johnson]': *BBC Five Live*, 1 January 2006.

CHAPTER 4: SPORT, HATRED AND THE CASE OF GOLF

'We dread them …': John Updike, *Golf Dreams* (London:
Penguin, 1996), p. 143.

'[hate] … integral part of supporting': 'Why can't footy fans just support their own team', http://answers.yahoo.com/question/index?qid=20070722141455AAd9UlT. For similar discussions see: http://soccerlens.com/are-you-a-true-football-fan/1559/, or http://commentisfree.guardian.co.uk/ciaran_jenkins/2006/05/why_i_hate_england.html.

'The results of this investment in fanaticism …': Matthew Yeomans, 'Soccer Inc: Marketing Fanaticism', *National Geographic*, June 2006.

'40 people hospitalised … [Old Firm]': 'Scotland's Secret Shame', *BBC Panorama*, 27 February 2005.

'The time for sitting idly by …': Rangers Supporters' Trust, 'Rangers trust urges Rangers fans to complain about Speirs', http://www.followfollow.com/news/loadnews.asp?cid=TMNW&id=257473, 22 December 2005.

'supporters threatened Spiers …': Brian Viner, 'Brave Prophet Spreads the Word against Rangers' Bile', *Independent*, 7 August 2007.

'Liverpool and United fans … [comparative statistics]': SportsWise, 'The FA Premier League National Fan Survey', for the 2002/03 and 2006/07 seasons.

'It's an initiative with soul …': *International Herald Tribune*, 12 September 2006.

'To say that it is more than a club …': Stephen Burgen, 'Charity Begins at the Nou Camp', *The Times*, 11 September 2006.

'Supporters of Barça want nothing …': Foer, *How Football Explains the World*, p. 191.

'Laporta is a Catalan … [players asked to learn language]': Duncan Shaw, 'Barcelona Player Raises Hackles with his Politics', Sapa-dpa, September 2007.

'[Inter] … anti-globalisation movement': Foer, *How Football Explains the World*, p. 185.

'The game of rugby is almost wholly devoid …': Rod Liddle, 'A Game Devoid of Skill', *Spectator*, 5 September 2007.

'[golf] … is the most honest': Rick Arnett, 'An Honest Sport: While other sports have problems, golf remains clean', *Sports Illustrated*, 26 August 2005.

'Italian professional golfer tested positive ...': BBC, 1 August 2007.

'Gary Player ... [negative reaction to doping comments]': Tom English, 'Dopey Reaction to Drugs Allegations', *Scotland on Sunday*, 22 July 2007.

'It'll almost feel like cheating ...': See, http://www.citygolfboston.com/.

'World's Top 100 ... [golfers]': 'Official World Golf Rankings', www.golf365.com, 22 October 2007.

'In oil-rich Gulf states, a new craze ...': Paul Ash, 'The Sultans of Bling', *Sunday Times*, Johannesburg, 19 March 2006.

'WWJD ... [Christian golfers]': For a detailed discussion of the marriage between religion and pro-golf in the US see Bruce Selcraig, 'America's Republican Guard', *The Irish Times*, 15 September 2006.

CHAPTER 5: SPORT, LIES AND SELF-DECEIT

'What luck for the rulers ... [Hitler]': As quoted in Ronald Wright, *A Short History of Progress*, (Edinburgh: Canongate, 2005), p. 130.

'Let's Blitz Fritz ...': As quoted in Luke Harding, 'The (Tabloid) War is Over: England, Germany and the World Cup, 2006', Anglo-German Foundation for the Study of Industrial Society, December 2006.

'[Torre and media] ... downright silly': George Kimball, 'America at Large', *The Irish Times*, 12 October 2006.

'Today a spectre haunts the editorial floor ...': Ian Jack ed., *The Granta Book of Reportage*, third edition, (London: Granta, 2006), pp. viii–ix.

'Manchester United ... [relationship with media]': *The Irish Times*, 4 November 2006.

'You've no right to ask that question ... [Motty]': Ibid.

'My job is to keep us out of the press ...': Ian Ladyman, 'The Fergie Manifesto,' *Daily Mail*, 31 July 2007.

'[Keane on van Nistelrooy] … fiddling': Daniel Taylor, 'United Pulled Earlier Keane Tape', *Guardian*, 4 November 2005.

'Sports reporters watched the footie …': Andrew Jennings, *Foul! The Secret World of Fifa* (London: HarperSport, 2006), p. 317.

'Ferguson said he planned never to speak to the BBC again …': *Guardian*, 6 September 2007.

'[Keys] … United have got two games': As quoted in Mary Hannigan, 'TV View', *The Irish Times*, 12 December 2005.

'The most watched TV programme in Australia …': OzTAM ratings 2000-2006.

'It was a downpayment on legend …': John Roberts, 'George Best was reliable only when there was a football at his feet', *Independent*, 26 November 2005. Another memory of the game can be found at: http://www.bbc.co.uk/fivelive/sport/best/index2.shtml.

'The trouble with nostalgia … [Parkinson]': Winner, *Those Feet*, p. 97.

'The Yale men had forced the ball … [Harding Davis]': Morgan, Meier and Schneider eds., *Ethics in Sport*, p. 74.

'You are a great champion … [Mayorga]': Associated Press, 'De la Hoya flattens then forgives Mayorga', 8 May 2006.

'All sports are being analysed …': *The Irish Times*, 27 December 2005.

'[Pires] … moment of madness': David Lacey, 'Arsenal Survive the Folly of Pires', *Guardian*, 24 October 2005.

'[golfers] … seriously well paid': Kevin Mitchell, 'Golfers Earn a Fortune for Losing', *Guardian*, 18 August 2006.

'Australia v New Zealand 1981 test match … [grubber]': Ben Schott, *Schott's Sporting, Gaming and Idling Miscellany*, (London: Bloomsbury, 2004), p. 121.

'workhorse Roger Hunt …': Winner, *Those Feet*, p. 32.

'[Cardiff stadium] … Coliseum': http://news.bbc.co.uk/1/hi/wales/461541.stm.

'[Magnusson] … a Spurs fan': *Daily Mail*, 21 November 2006.

'In some ways I admire football fans … [Jordan]': Andrew Fifield, 'On the Premiership', *The Irish Times*, 9 April 2007.

'fantasy leagues … [baseball court case]': *New York Times*, 16 May 2007.

'Fifa launched a purge … [lederhosen]': Luke Harding and Andrew Culf, 'Fifa Annoys Fans to Placate Sponsors', *Guardian*, 23 June 2006.

'FA outlawed … [Chelsea celery]': *Guardian*, 16 March 2007.

'We play football for money …': Trevor Phillips, Talk Radio 702, Johannesburg, May 2007.

'AFC Wimbledon … [match attendances]': AFP, 'Wimbledon rising from the ashes', 14 August 2007.

'Shareholders United vowed mass demonstrations …': *Independent on Sunday*, 15 May 2005.

'Two Middlesborough fans overheard …': Harry Pearson, 'All that Expense for Nothing', *Guardian*, 12 May 2006.

'Few signs are more odious …': Updike, *Golf Dreams*, p. 13.

'[Zidane and] … the distinct feeling of driving about 50 per cent …': John Waters, 'What Sport Teaches us about Life', *The Irish Times*, 3 July 2006.

'A psychologist at Georgia State University took saliva samples …': James C. McKinley Jr, 'It Isn't Just a Game', *New York Times*, 11 August 2000.

'Quebecois males aged 15 to 34 were more likely to kill themselves …': Frank Trovato, 'The Stanley Cup of Hockey and Suicide in Quebec, 1951-1992', *Social Forces*, Vol. 77, No. 1, September 1998. pp. 105–126

'Routinely reaching the playoffs …': Robert Fernquist, as summarised in Simon Kuper, 'A Matter of Life and Death, After All', *Financial Times*, 7 October 2005.

'British men unhappier in their 30s and 40s …': Defra, '2007 survey of public attitudes and behaviours toward the environment', 14 August 2007.

'People don't go to church as often …': As quoted in Sid Kirchheimer, 'Why the Super Bowl matters', http://www.webmd.com/balance/features/why-super-bowl-matters, WebMD, 2004.

'the psychologist Jon Kabat-Zinn once demonstrated ...': Richard
    Layard, *Happiness: Lessons from a new science*, (London: Allen
    Lane, 2005), pp. 187–8.

'I saw a car with the licence plate ARW 357 ...': Richard P.
    Feynman, *Six Easy Pieces*, (London: Penguin, 1998), p.xix.

'Life presents itself first and foremost as a task ...': Arthur
    Schopenhauer, *On the Suffering of the World*, (London:
    Penguin Great Ideas, 2004), p. 19.

'Join [us] ... to boost your entertainment ...': www.sky.com.

'What would my life be like without swimming ...': AFP,
    21 November 2006.

'[sport] ... offers people something to pay attention to ...': Noam
    Chomsky, *Manufacturing Consent*, (New York: Pantheon,
    1988).

'Their verdict re cherry-colour ball ...': *The Irish Times*,
    30 December 2006.

'We have developed a sort of compunction ...': As cited in
    Christopher Hitchens, *Orwell's Victory*, (London: Penguin,
    2003), p. 153.

'Instead of judging the job ... [sports chatter]': Peter Pericles
    Trifonas, *Postmodern Encounters: Umberto Eco and Football*,
    (London: Icon Books, 2001), pp. 57–8.

'deluxe cars and buses and flats ... (for Korean team)': Reuters, 26
    September 2006.

'The Lottery, with its weekly pay-out of enormous prizes ...':
    George Orwell, *Nineteen Eighty-four*, (London: Secker and
    Warburg, 1949).

'Electro-magnetic Golf ...': Aldous Huxley, *Brave New World*,
    (London: Penguin Modern Classics, 1969), p. 77.

'Superbowl attracted close to 100 million viewers ...':
    TV statistics from: *The Age*, 12 April 2005; *San Francisco
    Chronicle*, 22 March 2003; Reuters, 'Sport events dominate big
    global TV audiences', 30 December 2005.

Chapter 6: Sport, Conflict and Prejudice

'Sport is an instrument to help create a better world …': BBC
World, 'A Sporting Chance', April 2006.

'[Sport] … will help save humankind': Ibid.

'As we proceed on our way towards 2010 … [Mbeki]': Address at
African Union Summit, Ethiopia, 27 January 2007.

'few sports optimists/evangelists quote the first half of Orwell's
statement …': Sugden, 'Sport and Community Relations', in
Bairner ed., *Sport and the Irish*, p. 241.

'Serious sport has nothing to do with fair play …': G. Orwell,
'The Sporting Spirit', *Tribune*, London, December 1945.

'troops at Flanders came out of their trenches and [allegedly]
played …': Some debate over the veracity of the Christmas
truce game can be found at Simon Kuper, 'When Football
Brought Peace to the Trenches', 26 December 2003.

'Sport can help bridge cultural and ethnic divides … [IOC]':
www.olympic.org.

'[Fifa] … making the world a better place through football':
www.fifa.com.

'our [collective] work for the good of the world's young …':
Andrew Jennings, 'Manipulating Madiba', *Mail and Guardian*,
Johannesburg, 12 May 2006.

'the ability of sport, in particular football, to cross boundaries
…': Maria Bobenrieth, corporate responsibility director for
Nike, as quoted in Homeless World Cup press statement,
28 September 2006.

'The World Cup makes us in the UN green with envy …': Kofi
Annan, 'Football Envy at the UN', *Guardian*, 16 June 2006.

'Sport is the last hope for them … [Ogi]': BBC World, April 2006.

'black day for Hitler …': Alan English ed., *The Sunday Times:
Great Sporting Moments*, (London: HarperCollins, 2001).

'[Berlin] … the setting for great exploits': www.olympic.org.

'I think the writers showed bad taste …': Nick Pitt, 'Black Day for
Hitler', *The Sunday Times: Great Sporting Moments*, p. 47.

'Under the misleading heading "no discrimination" …':
http://www.olympic.org/uk/games/past/innovations_
uk.asp?OLGT=1&OLGY=1936.

'Had the Games been boycotted …': Guy Walters, *Berlin Games:
How Hitler stole the Olympic dream*, (London: John Murray,
2006), p. 93.

'[Francie Barrett] … still complained about being barred': 'Boxer
Takes Legal Advice', *The Irish Times*, 21 March 1998.

'[Algerian women] … subjected to discrimination in law and
practice': Amnesty International Annual Report, 2005.

'[Osama] … his affection for the game': *The Age*, 31 May 2002.

'Our racists say, "If only all Arabs could be like Zidane" …': As
quoted in *Financial Times*, 21 July 2007.

'What happened to Cameroon …': UNDP, UN Human
Development Report, 2006.

'development through sport is one of the most promising
channels …': Address at the opening of the first International
Conference on Sport and Development, Magglingen,
Switzerland, 17 February 2003.

'[Fifa] … gives "tied aid"': See, for example, Fifa press statement,
'Football for Hope taken to new dimension – support for
27 additional projects worldwide', 10 July 2007.

'[Livingstone] … rehabilitated Nazi war criminals': Alan
Hubbard, 'He used to Hate Sport', *Independent*, 31 August
2003. Also, 'Bagehot: The Chancer', *The Economist*, 13 January
2007.

'… fall-off in tourism to the Caribbean': 'Stumped',
The Economist, 3 May 2007.

'The economic arguments … are largely spurious': *The Economist*,
3 July 2004.

'When the Springboks went on to win the match …': Martin
Meredith, *The State of Africa*, (London: The Free Press, 2005),
p. 653.

'By and large, the white community … (Tutu)': BBC, 1 May 2006.

'The sense of unity was not real …': Interview with the author,
October 2007.

'… an orchestrated media affair': A. Grundlingh, 'From Redemption to Recidivism? Rugby and change in South Africa during the 1995 Rugby World Cup and its aftermath', *Sporting Traditions*, Vol. 14, No. 2, May 1998.

'If there is to be a relationship between rugby and the black majority …': Stephen Jones, 'Rainbow Warriors', *The Sunday Times: Great Sporting Moments*, p. 203.

'For some coaches SA Rugby's commitment …': 'SA Rugby Plays Dirty', *Noseweek*, October 2006.

'[Nigeria] … so many violent disputes broke out': Meredith, *The State of Africa*, p. 587.

'When Iraq won the Asian Cup …': 'A Winning Goal then back to War', *The Economist*, 4 August 2007.

'… my hero-worship of Banks was an important factor': Don Mullen, *Gordon Banks: A hero who could fly*, (Dublin: A Little Book Company, 2006), p. 67.

'football played an especially prominent role in the former Yugoslavia …': A lively discussion on football and the Balkan war can be found in the chapter on 'The Football Association laws' in Melvyn Bragg, '*The Great Unread: 12 books that changed the world*', (London: Hodder & Stoughton, 2006).

'[BUF] … adopted sports fanaticism as a cornerstone of its identity': Tony Collins, 'Return to Manhood: The cult of masculinity and the British Union of Fascists', in J.A. Mangan ed., *Superman Supreme: Fascist body as political icon*, (London: Frank Cass, 2000).

'The only methods we shall employ will be English ones …': Ibid, p. 157.

'Newspapers on both sides waged a campaign of hate …': Ian Jack ed., *The Granta Book of Reportage*, p. 24.

'Every now and then sport does marginal good or harm …': *Financial Times*, 8 November 2005.

'Euro '96 saw a resurgence … also saw a Russian student being stabbed': Winner, *Those Feet*, pp. 86–7, 119.

'Wandering among lunatic fans …': Foer, *How Football Explains the World*, p. 5.

'We saw the Minister out of courtesy … [Agar]': Neil Macfarlane, *Sport and Politics: A world divided*, (London: Willow Books, 1986), p. 142.

'Peter Hain recalled that some of the worst beatings …': Peter Hain, *Don't Play with Apartheid*, (London: George Allen and Unwin, 1971).

'[Brundage] … two savage attacks': As quoted in Robert Lipsyte, 'Evidence Ties Olympic Taint to 1936 Games', *New York Times*, 21 February 1999.

'Australian Peter Norman…': AFP, 'Superb Athlete Remembered for Protest', 4 October 2006.

'The International Cricket Council threatened to fine Australia …': Reuters, 4 May 2007.

'Uefa *did* fine Robbie Fowler …': Reuters, 27 March 1997.

'In 2000, the world footballing body told Brazil …': Jennings, *Foul!*, p. 240.

'In 2006, Fifa similarly told the government of Trinidad …': Ibid, p. 322.

'the Polish government suspended a number of officials [Fifa]': AFP, 7 March 2007.

'Politics and sport always mix. In grants …': Tom Humphreys, *Booked!* (Dublin: TownHouse, 2004), pp. 222–3.

'Scoring in the soccer love shack …': *Deutsche Welle*, 10 June 2005.

'Prostitutes work overtime …': Pravda.ru, 19 June 2006.

'one campaign group claimed that as many as 40,000 illegal immigrants …': Estimate given by the Parliamentary Assembly of the Council of Europe, as cited in Amnesty International press statement, 26 April 2006. Bruno Waterfield disputes the figures at: http://www.spiked-online.com/index. php?/site/article/2850/.

'[South Africa] … are considering legalising prostitution': *Cape Argus*, 30 March 2007.

'Let the women play in more feminine clothes …': BBC, 16 January 2004; http://news.bbc.co.uk/sport1/hi/ football/3402519.stm.

'[Cope] … typical of a bloke': Ibid.

'Companies could make use of a sweaty, lovely looking girl …':
    BBC, 17 June 2005.

'[Hammerettes] … snapped up by London neighbours': 'More
    Woe for West Ham', *Metro*, 12 February 2007.

'[Krajicek] … lazy, fat pigs': Gordon Thomson, 'The Worst
    Sporting Diplomats,' *Observer*, 2 March 2003.

'It is no use saying that other companies will emerge …':
    Macfarlane, *Sport and Politics*, p. 189.

'Heineken illustrated how companies … [Rugby World Cup]':
    Reuters, 14 September 2007.

'Is it not a monstrous interference with the liberty …': Bairner
    ed., *Sport and the Irish*, p. 12.

'I'd rather be a Paki …': 'Racism Shame for Hammers', *Mirror*,
    6 March 2007.

'When tennis legend Billie Jean King was outed … [Navratilova]':
    Clinton van der Berg, 'Gay Ref Blows Open Rugby's Closet
    Door', *Sunday Times*, Johannesburg, 29 July 2007.

'If one in 10 people are gay …': David James, 'Will a Gay
    Footballer ever come out of the Comfort Zone?', *Observer*,
    15 April 2007.

'[Humble] … tiny drop of water on an enormously big boulder':
    Interview with the author, August 2007. For figures on
    'retired' racehorses see also Antony Barnett, 'The Slaughtered
    Horses that Shame our Racing', *Observer*, 1 October 2006.

'[Western Cape] … funding was withdrawn': *Pretoria News*,
    27 April 2007.

'The funding was later reinstated … after the SPCA assured the
    owners': Alan Perrins, chief executive, Cape SPCA, interview
    with the author, July 2007.

'There are people who are concerned about the reputation of the
    sport … [Humble]': Interview with the author, July 2007.

'Fifteen minutes later they came back …': Bernard E. Rollin,
    'Rodeo and Recollection – Applied Ethics and Western
    Philosophy', in Morgan, Meier and Schneider, *Ethics in Sport*,
    p. 334.

Conclusion

'Those of the 207 Fifa member associations present …': Fifa media statement, 'Fifa President Joseph S. Blatter re-elected by acclamation', 31 May 2007.

'[Fifa] … supreme body': Ibid.

'One in five people … watched some of the 2006 Fifa World Cup': Fifa media statement, 6 February 2007.

INDEX

The New Rome
The Fall of an Empire and the Fate of America
Cullen Murphy

The rise and fall of ancient Rome has always been a metaphor for America, but here Cullen Murphy ventures past the obvious, bringing the brutal colours of Rome and the complexities of today's USA together in this beautifully written, intelligent and hugely readable book.

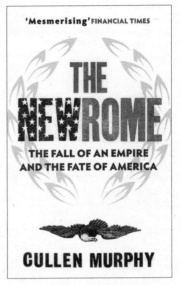

He explores how the two populations saw their political elites, and the insular cultures of Washington and Rome. He looks at the consequences of military overstretch and the widening gap between military and civilian society. Murphy sees both states weakened through 'privatisation' and vexed by the paradoxical issue of borders. Pressingly, he argues that America most resembles Rome in the burgeoning corruption of its government and in its arrogant ignorance of the world outside; in these conditions, idealism, however well-meant, can too easily be a form of blindness.

Lively and richly peppered with historical stories, Murphy's book brings the ancient world to life, and casts today's biggest superpower in a provocative new light.

Praise for *The New Rome*:
'Provocative and lively' – *New York Times*
'A nuanced and convincing view' – *Esquire* (US)
'Mesmerising' – *Financial Times*

Hardback   UK £14.99
ISBN-13: 978-1840468-87-8

Can You Trust the Media?

Adrian Monck with Mike Hanley

The media dominates
our lives. We give more
time to viewing, surfing,
listening and reading
than we do to our
families and friends.
It's a relationship
supposedly built on
trust – and it's a
relationship currently in
crisis.

TV's fake phone-ins,
phoney footage from
royal reality shows,
reporters resorting
to phone-bugging to
get stories – is there
anything left in the
media we can believe?

As audiences wonder
which way to turn,
former TV news boss
and award-winning
journalist Adrian Monck
turns an insider's eye on the scandals that have sucked the
public's trust from the media.

Underneath it all he argues that as we dither about
trust, the media doesn't really care. Editors and proprietors
want your time, attention and money... and if the truth gets
stretched in the process, then so be it.

But in the interactive Internet world, is there anything we
can do about this? Online readers are increasingly shaping the
media they consume. But will this act as a bulwark against the
lies and liberties; or even spur those on top to pay attention
to the public debate? Can You Trust The Media? looks at
the forces that have shaped the news, and those that are
remaking it.

Hardback   UK £12.99   Canada $26.00
ISBN-13: 978-1840468-72-4

Surveillance Unlimited

How We've Become the Most Watched People on Earth

Keith Laidler

Your car is satellite-tracked, your features auto-identified on video, your emails, faxes and phone calls monitored. You are covertly followed via transmitters implanted in your clothes, via your switched-off mobile and your credit card transactions. Your character, needs and interests are profiled by surveillance of every website you visit, every newsgroup you scan, every purchase you make. Big Brother is here, quietly adding to your files in the name of government efficiency and the fight against organised crime and terrorism.

As Keith Laidler argues in this urgent, important book, the potential for abuse is far-reaching and formidable. Surveillance can indeed fight crime. But, he asks, at what price? If we want zero crime, can we accept its price of zero freedom? Is the deployment of such technologies even legal? What will be their effects on the fabric of society? And what can we do to prevent the worst excesses?

This book has the answers.

Paperback   UK £10.99   Canada $20.00
ISBN-13: 978-1840468-77-9

50 Facts You Need to Know: USA
A Tour Through the Real America
Stephen Fender

- For 38 years San Francisco had a freeway that ended in mid-air
- *Hot Rod* magazine, with over 7.5 million readers, is one of the most popular car publications in the world
- More than 37 million Americans live below official poverty guidelines

The United States of America is a country with 50 capital cities, few of which anyone can name; a nation with 65 million gun-owners and 35,000 gun deaths each year; a place where there's one car for every adult, and where twice as many people claim to go to church as actually do. One city in Kentucky elected a black Labrador as its mayor. The US produces a quarter of all CO_2 emissions, and has a population rising twice as fast as that of the EU. German could have been the national language. Republican states especially are generous givers to charity, and they have a world-beating welfare state – the military.

Stephen Fender presents a vibrant, proud and yet critical portrait of the world's most powerful but least understood nation. Whether you love it or hate it, are about to visit or just keen to know more, the USA is here to stay. These 50 facts are the essential alternative guide.

Praise for *50 Facts You Need to Know: USA*

'Stephen Fender knows more facts about America than anyone I've ever met, and he's put fifty of the most fascinating in his book.' – John Sutherland

Paperback   UK £10.99   Canada $22.00
ISBN-13: 978-1840468-84-7